A WHOLE LOTTA GAME

FROM RUCKER TO REVENUE
- BUILDING BUSINESS THE STREETBALL WAY

BY ADRIAN WALTON

DISCLAIMER

The advice contained in this material might not be suitable for everyone. The author designed the information to present her opinion about the subject matter. The reader must carefully investigate all aspects of any business decision before committing to him or herself. The author obtained the information contained herein from sources she believes to be reliable and from her own personal experience, but she neither implies nor intends any guarantee of accuracy. The author is not in the business of giving legal, accounting, or any other type of professional advice. Should the reader need such advice, he or she must seek services from a competent professional. The author particularly disclaims any liability, loss, or risk taken by individuals who directly or indirectly act on the information contained herein. The author believes the advice presented here is sound, but readers cannot hold her responsible for either the actions they take, or the risk taken by individuals who directly or indirectly act on the information contained herein.

Published by 1BrickPublishing
Printed in the United States
Copyright © 2025 by Adrian Walton
ISBN 979-8898560003

DEDICATION

To the Architects of Dreams:

GREG MARIUS The visionary who built more than a tournament—you built a stage where street legends could become icons. You saw what Rucker could be when others only saw what it was. Your genius created the platform that changed my life and countless others. The blueprint you left behind shows us all how to turn passion into legacy. Rest in power, knowing your work continues through every kid who picks up a ball in Harlem.

ALIMOE "THE BLACK WIDOW" Your legacy as "The Black Widow" inspired me to reach beyond the game, to become a role model for Harlem's youth. The way you moved, the way you carried yourself—it wasn't just about basketball, it was about pride, identity, and showing the world what Harlem produces. You taught me that our responsibility extends beyond the court, into the community that raised us. Sleep in peace, knowing your commitment to the next generation still guides my path every day.

To these kings who left us too soon but whose legacies tower over Harlem like skyscrapers—I dedicate this book. You showed me that the game is bigger than basketball. You showed me how to turn street fame into lasting impact.

This book is my tribute to what you built—demanding attention not for me, but for the lessons you taught me that I now pass to the next generation.

BUTTA WILL NEVER FORGET ABOUT Y'ALL! I'LL HOLLAAAA

DEDICATION REQUEST

Please share this book with every young hustler trying to turn their game into greatness, every kid from the concrete who dreams bigger than their circumstances, every coach who knows there's more to teach than just the X's and O's, every mentor searching for a way to connect with today's youth, every parent wanting to show their child that there are many paths to success, and especially with those who society has already counted out. This playbook isn't just for hoopers—it's for anyone who understands that the principles that build legends on the court can build empires in the boardroom. Pass it on like a perfect assist and watch how it multiplies.

TABLE OF CONTENTS

WELCOME TO THE COURT

The first time I stepped onto the concrete at Rucker Park, I wasn't looking to become a legend. I was just another Harlem kid with game, trying to make a name for myself. What I didn't realize then was that those summer days battling on that hallowed court would teach me lessons that would carry me far beyond basketball—lessons about life, business, and success that no classroom could ever provide.

For those who don't know, Rucker Park isn't just any basketball court. It's sacred ground. Located at 155th Street and 8th Ave in Harlem or Frederick Douglass Boulevard as those new to the town call it; It's where street meets pro, where reputations are made and broken in a single crossover, where the crowd's roar can either lift you to new heights or crush your spirit entirely. During what I call the "golden era"—my era—this was where magic happened.

"What made Rucker Park so legendary is the people, the atmosphere," I'll tell anyone who asks. "I've seen SportsCenter set up in there. I've never seen the President show up to a street ball tournament before. Kobe Bryant, may he rest in peace, Jamal Crawford, so many NBA players... Fat Joe, P. Diddy, Jay-Z—they all had teams in there."

Think about that for a minute. Players getting $20-30 million to play in the NBA would come to Rucker to test themselves on concrete. Stephon Marbury was on the Knicks, on the Phoenix Suns, and he was at every game. Jamal Crawford was with the Chicago Bulls and was at every game. Why? Because Rucker wasn't just basketball—it was culture, it was proving ground, it was the ultimate test of whether you were real or just talk.

For me, Rucker was my NBA. I didn't make it to that level professionally, but at Rucker, I shared the court with NBA All-Stars, legends, and icons. I earned my stripes and my nickname—"Whole Lotta Game"—through blood, sweat, and a whole lot of buckets. When the crowd started chanting my name, when the rappers and ballers and everyone who was anybody wanted to see me play, that was my championship moment.

But here's what I learned the hard way: The applause doesn't last forever.

"Rucker taught me that you know, not to always play for the applause," I often reflect. "Because again, when I stopped playing basketball, I seen that I wasn't treated the same as I was when I was playing. People use you for your talent, and when you don't have a talent to offer them anymore, it depends on what type of person you are, whether you can handle that or not."

Many of the street legends before me didn't have good endings to their stories. They got the love, they got the name, they got the respect—but you can't take any of that to the bank. You can't feed your family with a flashy nickname or stories about that time you crossed up an NBA player. And that realization hit me like a defensive center coming across the lane.

This is where my story diverges from those street ball narratives you've heard before. This book isn't just about how I became "A-Butta" or how

I earned my stripes at Rucker. It's about what comes next—how I took the principles I learned on the court and translated them into business moves, how I've continuously reinvented myself, and how I'm building something that will last longer than my highlights on YouTube.

Basketball and business mirror each other in ways most people never realize. The discipline, the strategy, the teamwork, the ability to read your opponent, the importance of preparation, the value of building the right squad—these principles work whether you're trying to win a tournament or launch a startup. The court is just a different kind of boardroom, with its own rules and language, but the fundamentals of success remain the same.

Throughout this book, I'm going to show you how to take what might seem like street knowledge and translate it into business power. I'll share the real lessons from my journey—not just the highlight reels, but the benching, the losses, the times I had to swallow my pride and reinvent my game. Because that's where the real growth happens.

This isn't about getting rich quick or famous fast. If that's what you're looking for, you've picked up the wrong book. This is about building something real, something that lasts, something that creates opportunities not just for yourself but for your family and your community.

The one thing I hope that people take away from this book is to see that never give up. I never really heard street ball stories have good endings. I never really heard street ball people really figuring out with the legendary status and the love that they get in the streets... we brag about all the people that we connected to and got love for us and respect for us, but we can't take none of that to the bank.

Young kings and queens, this book is my playbook for you. Whether you're dribbling on concrete courts in Harlem or hustling in the suburbs, whether basketball is your thing or you've never picked up a ball in your life, the game I'm about to break down for you is universal. It's about how you move in this world, how you build your brand, how you assemble your team, how you execute your vision, and most importantly, how you create a legacy that outlasts your playing days.

So, lace up. The game's about to begin, and I'm passing you the ball.

Let's show them we got a whole lotta game—on and off the court.

CHAPTER 1

THE TIP-OFF - FINDING YOUR VISION

"**M**y original vision as a young Hooper, especially when I stepped on the scene, was just to get a name. From hearing what Rucker was all about, you knew that the announcers up there was giving guys names, so I kind of like mindset wise, just wanted to come into Rucker and just get a name."

Every game starts with the tip-off—that moment when the ball goes up, and everything you've prepared for begins. But before you even step on the court, you need to know what you're playing for. You need a vision.

When I first started playing ball in Harlem, my vision was simple: get a name. That might sound shallow to some, but in the world I came from, a name meant everything. A name meant respect. A name meant opportunities. A name meant you existed beyond the blocks that raised you.

In business terms, you might call this "building brand awareness" or "establishing market presence." But in the streets, we just call it getting your name up. It's the first step in any journey—defining what success looks like for you.

SEEING BEYOND YOUR BLOCKS

Growing up in Harlem, I was surrounded by legends I couldn't touch. Names like Andre Barrett, Omar Cook, Kenny Satterfield, Talik Brown. These were the guys in my age bracket that the streets talked about. They went to Catholic schools. They played with the right AAU teams. They were in the top programs. Their path seemed mapped out, while mine felt like I was walking through the dark.

"Being able to see and hear what those guys were getting, that's kind of like what I strived for," I remember thinking. But I wasn't getting the recognition they got. I didn't have the resources they had. I wasn't fortunate enough to get a scholarship to go to Rice High School, which was my dream.

This is something every entrepreneur from modest beginnings understands. You see others with advantages—better connections, more startup capital, prestigious education—and it's easy to think the game is rigged against you. But that's when you have to adjust your vision.

THE POWER OF ISOLATION

The turning point in my journey came when I got the opportunity to play with Riverside Church and the Gauchos, two powerhouse AAU teams in New York City. That exposure helped me get to prep school, which changed my life completely.

"I had an opportunity to get away from New York City and went to Milford Academy up in Connecticut," I explain. "I just had the gym. I had the key to the gym all the time, and I think that was a major key for me—isolation. My isolation helped me get stronger. Helped me focus on getting better, and I didn't really have no distractions."

When I came back to New York City, I was playing people that everyone thought were better than me. Everybody knew that. But I was able to beat people 36 to 4 and make them quit. Why? Because I had gotten stronger mentally during that time of isolation.

In business, this is what we call focused development. It's when you remove yourself from the noise and distractions to sharpen your skills, develop your plan, and build your foundation. Every successful entrepreneur I know has gone through periods of isolation—working late nights when friends were partying, saying no to distractions that would pull them off course, investing time in themselves when nobody was watching.

"Isolation really helps you evolve and be able to get better in anything in life," I've learned. "A lot of us don't like to isolate, don't like to be alone. But sometimes the aloneness gives you a chance to put some pieces back together and come back even stronger."

BUSINESS LESSON: Create deliberate periods of isolation to develop your skills and vision without distraction. The quiet moments are often where the greatest growth happens.

FINDING YOUR "WHY"

As I got older and wiser, my vision evolved. It wasn't just about getting a name anymore—it was about what I would do with that name once I had it.

One of the hardest questions anyone will ask you in business or in life is: "What's your why?" Why are you doing what you're doing? What's driving you? What gets you out of bed when the grind gets tough?

If I were to give advice to someone trying to find their why, I'd start with this: "Know who you are."

That sounds simple, but it's the hardest work you'll ever do. I had to learn this the hard way. As a person looked at as a legend, where everybody knows you and you know everybody, sometimes you find yourself following others instead of leading your own path.

"I'm a ballplayer, I'm not a rapper, but I followed the rappers," I admit. "So I kind of got an attitude that rappers have that I didn't realize I wasn't supposed to have as a ball player. Rappers are about themselves. Ball players are about team."

I fell victim to that character, that attitude, and it kept me out of rooms I should have been in. My character and attitude determined whether I was in the room or out of it. I didn't realize this until I had to take a step back, get isolated again, and really learn who I was.

This is crucial in business. Your "why" has to align with who you truly are—not who you think you should be or who others expect you to be. When your business vision aligns with your authentic self, that's when magic happens. That's when you can sustain the grind through the tough times, because you're not just chasing money or fame—you're fulfilling your purpose.

BUSINESS LESSON: Your business vision must align with your authentic self. When what you do matches who you are, you can sustain through the hardest challenges.

THE PATIENCE GAME

Setting goals isn't just about figuring out what you want—it's about having the patience to wait for the right timing to get it.

"I set my goals by really taking my time," I share. "I've worked on my patience. And more importantly, I try not to force things that I would understand from building with God that is already for me."

I used to push and rush things because I knew certain people or had certain connections. I thought I could make things happen on my timeline. But what I've learned is that whatever's for you is never forced.

"If abundance is your birthright, you don't have to fight for it," as I like to say.

In business, this translates to strategic patience. Yes, you need to hustle. Yes, you need to put in the work. But you also need to recognize when to push and when to wait, when to move aggressively and when to let things develop organically.

I've seen too many entrepreneurs rush products to market before they were ready, or scale before their infrastructure could support it, or make partnerships out of desperation rather than strategic alignment. Patience isn't passive—it's strategic.

"Your timing versus God's timing is two different timings," I always say. "What's to come is better than what's going. If you give Him a shot... whatever it was that you wanted, when you learn patience, what God gave you, you knew it was 5-10 times better than what you could have expected."

BUSINESS LESSON: Strategic patience is knowing when to hustle and when to wait. The right opportunity at the wrong time is still the wrong opportunity.

THE HARLEM VISION

When I talk about vision, I have to talk about Harlem. Because Harlem shaped how I see the world and what I believe is possible.

"Harlem means a lot to me because it helped me see that because I grew up in poverty, I didn't have to have a poverty mindset," I reflect. "There's so much that I see in Harlem that you can be ashamed of and hurt by, but there's so much of Harlem that you could see, wow, I didn't realize that it had this much of an impact."

Harlem taught me that your vision can't be limited by your current circumstances. I've seen the best of both worlds there—people who made it and struggled, and people who made it and kept it going. Those examples showed me that it was possible to create a vision that transcended the blocks that raised me.

"Harlem is really about the strong surviving," I believe. "It's really about showing you what you could be capable of doing, really coming from the mud, really coming out of the dirt."

Your vision has to be bigger than your environment but rooted in what your environment has taught you. I wouldn't trade my Harlem upbringing for anything, because it gave me a perspective that can't be taught in business school—it showed me how to see opportunity where others see obstacles, how to create value where others see nothing of worth.

BUSINESS LESSON: Your background isn't a limitation—it's a unique perspective that can become your competitive advantage.

STAYING TRUE WHILE EVOLVING

As your vision grows and evolves, one of the hardest challenges is staying true to who you are while becoming who you need to be.

People always say, "Remember where you came from." But I think it's more about trusting who you are and where you're going. I stay true to who I am because of who I want to become.

"I believe that the more and more that I focus on trying to be a better Adrian and a more mature Adrian, I don't think people ever could be able to judge me," I explain. "I think I've always been judged based off of what I've allowed myself to put myself in those spaces and those times, the things that I've chose to do."

Now that I'm more conscious of looking at what I'm choosing to do, it speaks to my character and who I'm becoming. I'm more focused on who I'm becoming than what I've done or any mistakes I've made.

In business, your vision has to include not just what you want to build, but who you want to become in the process of building it. The best entrepreneurs grow themselves as they grow their enterprises. Your business is a reflection of you—all your strengths, all your weaknesses, all your values, all your blind spots.

"A lot of people fall victim to other people's success," I've observed. "I'm surrounded around a lot of success, and that can become easy... you see someone else successful, you wind up just wanting to be successful. And it didn't matter if the success came from money, not your talent, you just wanted to be attached to the money."

But that's not vision—that's just chasing. True vision comes from understanding the unique talent God gave you and leaning into that with everything you've got.

"God gave all of us a talent, and that's what I'm not running from anymore," I affirm. "My talent has always been wanting to see people win. Why? Because I always wanted to win."

BUSINESS LESSON: Your business vision should reflect your authentic talents and values, not just what seems profitable or popular.

CREATE YOUR VISION: THE PLAYBOOK

Now it's time for you to develop your own vision. Here's how to start:

1. **Isolate and Reflect:** Set aside dedicated time away from distractions to think deeply about what you truly want to build and why. This might be a weekend retreat, a daily morning routine before anyone else is awake, or regular sessions in a place that inspires you.

2. **Know Your Name:** What do you want to be known for? Not just now, but 5, 10, 20 years from now? Your name is your brand—define it intentionally.

3. **Identify Your Unique Talent:** What comes naturally to you that others struggle with? What do people consistently come to you for? That's your zone of genius—build your vision around that.

4. **Study Your Models:** Who has accomplished what you want to accomplish? Study them, but don't try to be them. Learn from their path, but chart your own.

5. **Define Success In Your Terms:** Success isn't just money or fame. Is it impact? Freedom? Creative expression? Family legacy? Be specific about what winning looks like for you.

6. **Write It Down:** A vision that stays in your head isn't a vision— it's a daydream. Write down your vision in clear, specific language. Make it tangible.

7. **Test Your Why:** Ask yourself, "If this got really hard and took twice as long as I expected, would I still want to do it?" If the answer is no, you haven't found your true why yet.

8. **Share It Strategically:** Don't tell everyone your vision, but do tell those who can help you refine it and achieve it. Their feedback will strengthen your clarity.

Remember, your first vision doesn't have to be your final vision. Mine certainly wasn't. It will evolve as you grow, as you learn, as you experience both wins and losses. The important thing is that you have a direction— something to move toward, something that pulls you forward when motivation fades.

Your vision is the first step in the game. Without it, you're just running up and down the court with no purpose. With it, every move you make brings you closer to the win.

Now, let's get to work. The ball is in your hands.

COURT TO BUSINESS: VISION APPLICATION

On the Court	In Business
Getting a name at Rucker	Building brand recognition in your market
Using isolation to develop skills	Creating focused time for skill development and planning
Understanding your role on the team	Identifying your unique value proposition
Reading the game before making a move	Market research before launching a product
Setting goals for your basketball career	Creating short and long-term business objectives
Adapting your game as you grow	Pivoting your business model as you learn

REAL TALK WITH A-BUTTA

I lost my first one-on-one game at age 33. The world saw me lose to Jesse Sapp. After that, I had to reinvent myself because I realized I didn't have all the love and connections I thought I had.

"I went and told myself that I was gonna change my ways and my looks of who I was," I remember deciding. "I felt like if people thought that all they was gonna ever see me was, and when they see me, just talk to me about basketball... I'm doing stuff to make you see about my life. Don't talk to me about basketball unless you see me doing something to help the tournament you want to coach in. I want to own."

I had to figure out how to reinvent myself to show that life after basketball could still be successful, just like it was for me on the basketball court. I started my podcast in 2016 and didn't get sponsorship until 2024. That's eight years of grinding with no guarantee it would pay off.

"Getting into a lane and doing something not really knowing... this entrepreneurship world versus really getting a job and having a 401(k), to really think about a retirement knowing you got kids—these choices ain't easy," I admit.

But the determination I always had on the court is the same mindset I have off the court. I've always told myself that if I became a legend on the court, there's no way you can tell me I can't become one off the court.

That's the kind of vision you need to have—one that sees beyond the current game into the next one, and the one after that. Because life is a tournament, not a single game. And the real champions are the ones who keep winning long after the crowd has gone home.

CHAPTER 2

COURT AWARENESS - READING THE GAME

"My *approach to basketball was always about preparation. My mindset was simple: failing to prepare is preparing to fail. You can't just show up and expect to win—you've got to put in the work before you even step on the court."*

In basketball, they call it court awareness—that almost supernatural ability to see the whole floor, to know where every player is moving, to anticipate the play before it happens. The greatest point guards don't just see what's happening now; they see what's going to happen three moves ahead.

In business, we call it market intelligence or strategic thinking. But it's the same skill: the ability to read the game as it unfolds and position yourself for success.

When I was coming up at Rucker, this wasn't something I learned in a classroom. I learned it through hours in the gym, through observation, through trial and error, through mentorship. And now I'm passing these lessons to you.

THE PREPARATION ADVANTAGE

My coaches used to drill into me: "Early is on time. On time is late. Late is unacceptable."

At first, I didn't get it. If practice started at 3:00, why did I need to be there at 2:30? But over time, I realized what they were really teaching me—preparation gives you an edge that talent alone can't provide.

"If you're not preparing, I would say that you're kind of like setting yourself up to get ready to deal with what I call loose ends," I explain now. "The more and more that you constantly sharpening your skills... you know, again, like I said, you could continue to do a podcast and just talk to people, and then you could eventually learn how to talk to people and then start doing business with them."

In business, this means doing your homework before you make a move. It means understanding your market before you launch your product. It means studying your competition before you position against them. It means knowing your customer's needs before you try to meet them.

The streets taught me that the unprepared get exposed quickly. In Harlem, if you step on a court unprepared, thinking your natural talent will carry you, you'll get embarrassed in front of everyone. The same principle applies in business. Natural talent might get you in the door, but preparation keeps you in the room.

BUSINESS LESSON: Preparation isn't just about avoiding failure—it's about creating opportunities that the unprepared never even see.

THE GYM RAT MENTALITY

I was what they called a "gym rat." My man Lex, who ran St. Mark's and worked at the wig store on 125th Street, he used to say, "Close to Lenox, you live on Seventh, you need to come down between Lenox and Fifth and live in this gym."

At the time, I didn't fully understand what he meant. But looking back, I realize he was teaching me that greatness requires obsession. You can't just want it casually. You have to be willing to live it, breathe it, sleep it.

"It was all someone saying, with your leisure time, do you want to get better?" I reflect now. "And they didn't want that to be on them, forcing that on me. They wanted me to want that for myself."

In business, this translates to immersing yourself completely in your industry. It means reading everything you can get your hands on about your market. It means attending events and networking relentlessly. It means studying successful business models and failed ones with equal intensity. It means staying on top of trends and ahead of changes.

The gym rat mentality isn't about working hard for a season and then coasting. It's about consistent, relentless improvement over time. It's about treating your business like a craft that you're constantly refining.

BUSINESS LESSON: Immerse yourself completely in your industry. The depth of your knowledge creates the height of your success.

SEEING WHAT OTHERS DON'T

What separated me on the court wasn't just physical ability. It was the ability to see openings others didn't, to recognize patterns in how defenders moved, to anticipate rather than just react.

This same skill is crucial in business. The most successful entrepreneurs don't just see the market as it is—they see opportunities that others miss. They spot gaps in the market. They identify unmet needs. They recognize trends before they become obvious.

When I look at business opportunities today, I try to spot patterns and connections that others might overlook. I ask questions like:

- Where are people experiencing frustration that nobody is addressing?
- What's working in one industry that could be applied to another?
- What behaviors are changing that might create new opportunities?
- Who is being underserved or ignored entirely?

This kind of awareness doesn't happen automatically. It comes from being observant, from asking questions, from staying curious, from removing yourself from the echo chamber and looking at situations with fresh eyes.

BUSINESS LESSON: Train yourself to spot patterns and opportunities that others miss. The biggest opportunities often hide in plain sight.

THE MENTAL GAME

Many people don't realize how much of basketball is mental rather than physical. The same is true in business.

"Everybody's training kids today, but the game is more mental than any physical you could do," I often point out.

What does this mean practically? It means understanding psychology—both your own and others'. It means recognizing how emotions affect decisions. It means maintaining focus when distractions arise. It means staying confident through slumps and humble through success.

In business, the mental game shows up in your ability to:

- Stay calm during negotiations
- Make decisions based on data rather than emotion
- Persist through rejection and setbacks
- Manage your energy and avoid burnout
- Control your narrative and not let others define you
- Trust your preparation when pressure moments arise

I've seen incredibly talented players crumble under pressure because they hadn't developed mental toughness. I've seen average players elevate their game in crucial moments because they had mastered their mindset. The same dynamic plays out in business every day.

BUSINESS LESSON: Your mindset is as important as your skill set. Mental preparation creates resilience when challenges arise.

STUDYING YOUR OPPONENTS

In basketball, you study film to understand your opponents' tendencies. You want to know: Do they always drive right? Do they have a weak crossover? Do they lose confidence after missing a few shots?

In business, studying your competition is just as crucial. But many entrepreneurs skip this step. They're so focused on their own product or service that they don't take time to truly understand what they're up against.

Effective competitor analysis isn't about copying what others do—it's about understanding the landscape so you can position yourself strategically. It's about finding the weaknesses in their game that create openings for yours.

When I analyze competitors today, I look at:

- What they do well (so I don't waste time trying to beat them at their strength)
- What they neglect (which might indicate an opportunity)
- Who they serve (and more importantly, who they don't)
- How they talk about themselves (to find positioning opportunities)
- Their business model (to potentially innovate on how value is delivered)

Just like in basketball, the goal isn't to obsess over your opponents. The goal is to understand them well enough that you can play your own game more effectively.

BUSINESS LESSON: Study your competition not to imitate them, but to find the gaps they've left open for you to exploit.

READING THE CULTURE

At Rucker, understanding the game meant more than just understanding basketball. It meant understanding the culture—the crowd, the announcer, the music, the whole atmosphere. Players who could read and respond to that cultural context had an advantage over those who couldn't.

In business, cultural awareness is equally important. Markets exist within cultural contexts that are constantly evolving. Entrepreneurs who can read these cultural shifts—and respond to them appropriately—have a significant edge.

"I try not to bring people outside of where they would have to work or do a little bit more than who they are," I explain when talking about collaborations. This shows cultural intelligence—understanding people's authentic zones and not forcing them into spaces that don't align with who they are.

This same principle applies to understanding your market. You need to recognize:

- The values that drive your audience's decisions
- The language and references that resonate with them
- The influences that shape their perspective
- The trends that are gaining momentum
- The pain points that aren't being addressed

Cultural intelligence isn't about superficial trends—it's about deeper understanding of human motivation and behavior. It's about recognizing not just what people do, but why they do it.

BUSINESS LESSON: Business doesn't happen in a vacuum. Understanding the cultural context of your market creates opportunities for deeper connection and relevance.

THE POWER OF OBSERVATION

One of the most underrated skills in both basketball and business is simple observation. Not just looking, but truly seeing.

When I was developing my game, I would watch players like Charles Jones (a two-time NCAA scoring champion), his brother Lamont Jones (a true natural point guard), Kareem Reed, and Stefan Marbury. I didn't just admire their highlights—I studied how they approached the game, how they made decisions, how they created opportunities.

"I didn't realize, until I look back, that I was always playing with people that were like-minded as me, that wanted, that wanted to and knew how to win," I reflect now.

The same skill applies to business. The most successful entrepreneurs are keen observers. They don't just study business books or listen to podcasts—they watch how successful businesses operate. They notice details that others miss. They reverse-engineer strategies that work. They learn from failures as well as successes.

Observation isn't passive—it's an active skill that you can develop:

- Be specific about what you're looking for
- Take notes on patterns you notice
- Ask questions about why things work the way they do
- Consider multiple perspectives on the same situation
- Look for principles that can be applied across contexts

BUSINESS LESSON: Cultivate the habit of structured observation. Study success patterns that you can adapt to your own business.

CREATING YOUR BUSINESS INTELLIGENCE SYSTEM: THE PLAYBOOK

Now it's time to develop your own court awareness in business. Here's how to build a system that keeps you informed and ahead of the game:

1. **Market Monitoring Routine:** Set aside dedicated time each week to stay current on your industry. Create a list of sources—newsletters, publications, podcasts, YouTube channels, industry reports—that keep you informed. Make this non-negotiable.

2. **Competitor Analysis Framework:** Create a simple system to track 3-5 key competitors. Document their offerings, pricing, messaging, customer feedback, and recent moves. Update this quarterly to spot patterns and shifts.

3. **Customer Listening Posts:** Establish regular ways to hear directly from customers—surveys, interviews, social media monitoring, review analysis. The goal is to understand their evolving needs and pain points before your competition does.

4. **Trend Tracking System:** Identify 3-5 broader trends that could impact your business. These might be technological, social,

economic, or regulatory. Monitor how these trends are developing and brainstorm how they might create opportunities.

5. **Network Intelligence:** Build relationships with people who have different perspectives on your industry—suppliers, distributors, adjacent businesses, industry veterans. Schedule regular conversations to gain insights you wouldn't get from public sources.

6. **Reflection Routine:** Don't just collect information—make sense of it. Schedule monthly review sessions where you connect dots between what you're observing and what it means for your business.

7. **Decision Triggers:** Based on your intelligence gathering, identify specific conditions that would trigger decisions—when to launch new offerings, when to adjust pricing, when to enter new markets, when to pivot your approach.

Remember, the goal isn't just to collect information—it's to develop insight that leads to action. Many businesses suffer from information overload but insight underload. The difference between the two is reflection and meaning-making.

COURT TO BUSINESS: AWARENESS APPLICATION

On the Court	In Business
Studying opponents' tendencies	Competitive analysis to identify market opportunities
Recognizing defensive patterns	Identifying barriers to entry and how to overcome them

Reading the referee's style	Understanding regulatory environment and working within it
Feeling the crowd's energy	Gauging market sentiment and timing launches accordingly
Knowing team-mates' strengths	Understanding your team's capabilities and gaps
Anticipating plays before they happen	Predicting market shifts based on early indicators

REAL TALK WITH A-BUTTA

One of the hardest things to learn in business is that information alone isn't enough. You have to act on what you know.

"It's hard to explain, but only those that are in that world and like-minded like that, you would understand that whatever it was that you wanted, when you learn patience, what God gave you, you knew it was 5-10 times better than what you could have expected," I share.

This is the balance you have to find—between gathering intelligence and taking action. Between preparation and execution. Between planning and doing.

Too many entrepreneurs get stuck in analysis paralysis. They keep researching, keep planning, keep preparing—but never pull the trigger. Others rush in without doing their homework and get burned because they didn't read the situation correctly.

Finding that balance comes with experience, but it also comes from trusting your preparation. When you've done the work to understand your market, when you've studied the patterns, when you've built the skills—at some point, you have to trust that and make your move.

That's what separates players from spectators, entrepreneurs from dreamers. The willingness to take what you've learned from reading the game and put it into action, knowing that you've prepared as best you can for whatever comes next.

The court is waiting. The ball is in your hands. You've studied the defense. Now it's time to make your move.

CHAPTER 3

HANDLES - MASTERING FUNDAMENTAL SKILLS

"I *was just a person that worked. I was a gym rat. My coach gave me the key to the gym, and I practically lived there. That's what separated me—while others were out doing whatever, I was in that gym working on my fundamentals over and over until they became automatic."*

In basketball, your handles are everything. If you can't control the ball, you can't control the game. The players with the tightest handles—the ones who can move the ball like it's an extension of their own body—they're the ones who create opportunities not just for themselves, but for their entire team.

The same principle applies in business. Your fundamental skills are your handles. They're the basic capabilities that everything else builds upon. Without them, all the strategy and vision in the world won't get you where you want to go.

THE FUNDAMENTALS FIRST MINDSET

When I was coming up, a lot of young players wanted to start with the flashy moves. They wanted to do the crossovers and behind-the-back passes before they mastered the basics. But that approach creates gaps in your game that get exposed when the pressure is on.

I learned early that the fundamentals aren't glamorous, but they're essential. Dribbling drills. Footwork. Defensive stance. Proper shooting form. These basics might not make the highlight reel, but they're what separate the players from the pretenders.

In business, your fundamentals are skills like:

- Financial literacy – understanding the numbers that drive your business
- Communication – being able to clearly articulate your ideas and listen effectively
- Time management – making the most of your most limited resource
- Problem-solving – approaching challenges with a structured process
- Relationship building – creating genuine connections with customers, partners, and team members

These skills might not seem as exciting as raising capital or launching products, but they're the foundation everything else rests on. When the business equivalent of a full-court press comes, it's your fundamentals that will see you through.

BUSINESS LESSON: Master the basics before pursuing the advanced. Strong fundamentals create the foundation for everything else.

THE DAILY DRILL

When I talk about being a gym rat, I'm talking about putting in work every single day. Not when I felt like it. Not when it was convenient. Every. Single. Day.

My daily routine wasn't glamorous. It was repetitive. The same drills, the same movements, over and over until they became second nature. Three hundred jump shots. Ball-handling drills. Defensive slides. I did them until my body knew the movements better than my mind did.

In business, this translates to daily practice of your core skills. If communication is fundamental to your business, you practice it daily—writing clearly, speaking persuasively, listening actively. If financial management is key, you review your numbers daily, not just at the end of the month. If customer service is central, you practice those interactions until your approach is both natural and exceptional.

The key is consistency and deliberate practice. It's not just about putting in time—it's about focused improvement, about identifying weaknesses and addressing them systematically, about pushing yourself just beyond your current capabilities so that growth happens.

BUSINESS LESSON: Success is built through daily discipline, not occasional inspiration. Identify your core skills and practice them deliberately every day.

IDENTIFYING YOUR WEAK SPOTS

Every player has strengths and weaknesses. The great ones are honest about both.

When I was developing my game, I had to acknowledge where I was weak. My left hand wasn't as strong as my right. My mid-range jumper needed work. Once I identified these gaps, I could focus my practice time on strengthening them.

In business, this same honesty is crucial. Maybe you're great at product development but struggle with sales conversations. Maybe you understand marketing but get overwhelmed by financial projections. Maybe you're a visionary but have trouble with day-to-day execution.

These weaknesses don't make you a failure—they make you human. But leaving them unaddressed makes you vulnerable.

The process for addressing weak spots is straightforward:

1. Identify specific skills where you need improvement
2. Seek out resources to help you develop those skills (courses, books, mentors)
3. Create a deliberate practice plan
4. Measure your progress
5. Get feedback from others who can see your blind spots

Remember, the goal isn't perfection in every area. It's sufficiency in your weak areas and excellence in your strong ones.

BUSINESS LESSON: Honest self-assessment accelerates growth. Identify your weaknesses and address them systematically.

LEARNING FROM THE MASTERS

I didn't develop my game in isolation. I studied the masters. I watched how they moved, how they created space, how they made decisions. I didn't just admire their highlights—I analyzed how they achieved those results and then incorporated those lessons into my own game.

In business, this means studying those who have mastered the skills you need. This could mean:

- Reading books by industry leaders
- Watching interviews and presentations by successful entrepreneurs
- Taking courses taught by proven experts
- Finding mentors who excel in areas where you struggle
- Examining case studies of businesses similar to yours

The key is to move beyond passive consumption to active learning. Don't just admire what others have accomplished—deconstruct how they did it. Look for the principles behind their success, not just the specific tactics they used.

And remember, you don't have to adopt someone else's entire approach. Take what works for you, adapt it to your own style and situation, and leave the rest.

BUSINESS LESSON: Stand on the shoulders of giants. Learn from those who have mastered the skills you need, but adapt their lessons to your unique situation.

THE SKILL OF ADAPTABILITY

One of the most important skills I developed was adaptability. Different courts, different opponents, different situations all required adjustments to my game. The player who can only play one way, who can only succeed under ideal conditions, has a ceiling on their potential.

In business, adaptability is becoming increasingly important as the pace of change accelerates. Markets shift. Technologies evolve. Customer preferences change. Regulations update. The business that can't adapt quickly becomes obsolete.

Adaptability isn't about abandoning your fundamentals—it's about applying them in changing contexts. It's about recognizing when conditions have shifted and adjusting your approach accordingly. It's about being willing to experiment and learn rather than clinging to what worked in the past.

This skill becomes particularly important as you grow. What works when you're a solo entrepreneur might not work when you have a team. What works in your local market might not work when you expand nationally. What works with early adopters might not work with the mainstream market.

BUSINESS LESSON: Build adaptability into your skill set. The business landscape is constantly changing, and your ability to adjust is as important as any other capability.

THE POWER OF REPETITION

When I think about skill development, one word comes to mind: repetition. The moves that served me best in crucial moments weren't the ones I practiced occasionally—they were the ones I had done thousands of times, in every possible variation, until they were completely automatic.

In business, this principle applies to your core processes. The activities that drive your success should become so familiar that you can execute them flawlessly even under pressure. This might include:

- Your sales conversation
- Your customer onboarding process
- Your content creation workflow
- Your financial review routine
- Your daily productivity system

The goal is to make these processes so ingrained that they don't require conscious thought, freeing up your mental energy for higher-level decisions and creative thinking.

This doesn't mean these processes never evolve—they should. But they evolve from a foundation of mastery, not as a reaction to poor execution.

BUSINESS LESSON: Build your critical business processes into habits through deliberate repetition. What you do consistently defines your results.

FROM MECHANICAL TO MAGICAL

When you first learn a skill, it feels mechanical. You have to think about each component, each movement. But with enough practice, something magical happens—the skill becomes fluid, natural, even artistic.

I experienced this transformation with my game. What started as mechanical drills eventually became fluid expression. The fundamentals didn't constrain my creativity—they enabled it. Once the basics were automatic, I could focus on creating, on seeing opportunities, on elevating my game.

The same progression happens in business. When you first learn to manage finances, create marketing campaigns, or have sales conversations, these activities feel mechanical and sometimes even awkward. But as you master them, they become second nature, allowing your unique style and creativity to shine through.

This is when your business transcends mere competence and begins to stand out. It's when the fundamentals you've mastered become the foundation for innovation rather than limitation.

BUSINESS LESSON: Mastery of fundamentals doesn't constrain creativity—it enables it. When basics become automatic, your unique approach can emerge.

DEVELOPING YOUR FUNDAMENTAL SKILLS: THE PLAYBOOK

Now it's time to develop your own business fundamentals. Here's a structured approach to building the skills that will support your success:

1. **Skills Audit:** Create an inventory of the fundamental skills needed in your business area. Be honest about your current level in each (beginner, intermediate, advanced). Prioritize 2-3 areas for focused improvement.

2. **Development Plan:** For each priority skill, identify specific resources to help you improve—books, courses, mentors, practice opportunities. Create a timeline for your development with clear milestones.

3. **Daily Practice Routine:** Block out time every day (even just 30 minutes) for deliberate practice of your fundamental skills. Be specific about what you'll work on and how you'll measure improvement.

4. **Feedback Loop:** Establish a system for getting regular feedback on your skills development. This could be from coaches, mentors, peers, or even customers. Use this feedback to refine your practice.

5. **Skill Integration:** Look for opportunities to apply your developing skills in real business situations. The transfer from practice to application is where true mastery begins.

6. **Progress Tracking:** Document your growth over time. Notice not just external results but also how the skills begin to feel more natural and require less conscious effort.

7. **Expansion Plan:** As you master one set of fundamentals, identify the next level of skills to develop. The journey of skill development never truly ends.

Remember, developing your fundamental skills isn't glamorous work. It happens in the quiet moments when no one is watching. It happens through consistent effort over time. But it's this invisible work that creates visible results when opportunity arrives.

COURT TO BUSINESS: SKILLS APPLICATION

On the Court	In Business
Dribbling fundamentals	Basic financial literacy and management
Shooting form	Core communication and presentation skills
Defensive stance	Customer service and relationship building
Court vision	Market analysis and opportunity identification
Physical conditioning	Personal productivity and energy management
Basketball IQ	Business model understanding and strategic thinking

REAL TALK WITH A-BUTTA

I wasn't born with a basketball in my hands. I was what they call a late bloomer—I didn't start playing seriously until I was 12 or 13, while guys like Andre Barrett and Kareem Reed might have started at 8 or 9.

But what I lacked in early start, I made up for in intensity. When I got to Milford Academy in Connecticut and had access to a gym all the time, I took full advantage. That isolation and focus helped me level up my game in ways that surprised people when I returned to New York.

Players who had always been better than me couldn't understand how I was suddenly beating them 36 to 4, making them quit mid-game. They didn't see the hours in the gym. They didn't see the repetitions. They didn't see the fundamentals being drilled until they became automatic.

They just saw the results.

That's how it works in business too. People see the success, but they don't see the skill development that preceded it. They don't see the late nights learning how to read financial statements. They don't see the sales pitches that bombed before the ones that landed. They don't see the marketing messages that failed before the ones that resonated.

They just see the results.

But you and I know the truth. We know that results aren't random—they're the product of fundamental skills developed consistently over time. We know that what looks like overnight success is actually years of preparation meeting opportunity.

So while others are looking for shortcuts and hacks, we're in the gym, working on our handles. Because when the big game comes—and it always does—it's not about who wants it more in that moment. It's about who has prepared for that moment every day leading up to it.

That's the secret that isn't really a secret at all. It's just the truth that most aren't willing to accept: There is no substitute for mastering the fundamentals.

So what are you working on today?

CHAPTER 4

THE CROSSOVER - CREATING YOUR PERSONAL BRAND

"*W*hen I stepped on the scene, I knew the announcers at Rucker *were giving guys names. I wanted to come into Rucker and just get a name. That name became my brand, my identity. But what I learned is that the name isn't enough—it's what you do with it that matters.*"

In basketball, the crossover is one of the most devastating moves in the game. When executed perfectly, it creates separation between you and your defender, opening up opportunities to score or make plays for your team. The best crossovers don't just work once—they become signature moves that opponents know are coming but still can't stop.

In business and life, your personal brand is your crossover. It's what separates you from everyone else in your field. It's what makes people remember you. It's what creates opportunities even when you're not in the room.

At Rucker, I became known as "A-Butta" and "Whole Lotta Game." Those names weren't just nicknames—they were brands that carried weight. They opened doors, created opportunities, and set expectations. But building and maintaining that brand was about much more than just having a catchy name.

FROM NAME TO BRAND

When I first hit the courts at Rucker, getting a name was everything. In that world, your name—your brand—was your currency. It determined whether people would come to see you play, whether teams would want you on their roster, whether opportunities would flow your way.

But I quickly learned that a name alone isn't enough. It's what you attach to that name that matters. It's the consistency of your performance, the uniqueness of your style, the values you demonstrate, the reputation you build.

In business, this translates directly to personal branding. Your name (or your company's name) is just the beginning. Your brand is the total experience people have with you—the quality of your work, how you communicate, the problems you solve, the values you embody, the way you make people feel.

A strong personal brand doesn't just happen. It's built intentionally through consistency, authenticity, and strategic positioning. It's the result of aligning who you are with how you present yourself to the world.

BUSINESS LESSON: Your brand goes far beyond your name. It's the total experience people have with you and the unique value you represent.

AUTHENTICITY OVER IMITATION

One of the biggest lessons I learned about building a name at Rucker was the importance of authenticity. Everyone wanted to be the next Stephon Marbury or the next Allen Iverson. But those positions were already taken. The players who made a lasting impression were the ones who brought something unique to the court—their own style, their own approach, their own personality.

"I'm a ballplayer, I'm not a rapper," I remind myself. "Rappers are about themselves. Ball players are about team." When I tried to adopt a rapper's mindset because I was hanging around rappers, it didn't align with who I really was, and it kept me out of rooms I should have been in.

In business, authentic branding is just as important. Too many entrepreneurs try to imitate the successful brands they admire rather than developing a brand that authentically represents their unique strengths and values. They use language that doesn't sound like them, create visuals that don't reflect their real style, or position themselves in markets that don't align with their true expertise.

Authentic branding isn't about fabricating an image—it's about strategically emphasizing the best of who you actually are. It's about finding the intersection between what you're genuinely good at, what you genuinely care about, and what your market genuinely needs.

BUSINESS LESSON: Build your brand on authentic strengths and values. Imitation might create short-term attention, but authenticity creates long-term trust.

CONSISTENCY CREATES CREDIBILITY

At Rucker, your name wasn't built on one great game. It was built on showing up consistently and delivering at a high level time after time. The players who couldn't be counted on—who were amazing one day and disappeared the next—never built the credibility that converted to real opportunities.

In business, consistency is just as crucial to your personal brand. It shows up in:

- The quality of your products or services
- How you communicate with customers
- The experience people have working with you
- Your follow-through on commitments
- The values you demonstrate in every interaction

Consistency doesn't mean you never evolve or improve. It means that certain core elements of your brand—your values, your quality standards, your unique approach—remain reliable even as you grow and develop.

This consistency creates trust, and trust is the foundation of every successful brand. People need to know what they can expect from you before they're willing to invest their time, attention, or money.

BUSINESS LESSON: Consistency is the bridge between branding and trust. Deliver on your brand promise reliably, and credibility will follow.

REPUTATION MANAGEMENT

Your name at Rucker wasn't just what the announcer called you—it was what people said about you when you weren't around. It was the reputation you built through your actions both on and off the court.

In today's business world, reputation management has become more important than ever. Your brand exists not just in your own marketing materials but in online reviews, social media conversations, customer testimonials, and word-of-mouth.

Managing that reputation isn't about controlling what everyone says—that's impossible. It's about consistently delivering experiences that generate positive feedback. It's about responding appropriately when issues arise. It's about being intentional about how you show up in every interaction.

I'm very conscious of how I represent myself because I've seen how quickly reputations can be damaged. "I think I've always been judged based off of what I've allowed myself to put myself in those spaces and those times, the things that I've chose to do," I reflect. "Now that I'm more conscious of looking at what I'm choosing to do, it speaks a little bit more on my character and who I'm becoming."

BUSINESS LESSON: Your brand isn't just what you say about yourself—it's what others say about you. Build a reputation through actions, not just words.

DIFFERENTIATION IN A CROWDED MARKET

Rucker Park was full of talented players. To stand out, you couldn't just be good—you had to be distinctive. You needed something that separated you from everyone else on the court, whether that was a unique skill, a signature move, or a playing style all your own.

The business world is equally crowded. In almost every category, customers have countless options. Building a strong personal brand requires differentiation—a clear articulation of what makes you different from and better than the alternatives.

Effective differentiation is:

- Relevant to your audience (it matters to them, not just to you)
- Demonstrable (you can prove it, not just claim it)
- Sustainable (you can maintain it over time)
- Difficult to copy (it's based on your unique combination of skills and attributes)

The key is to identify the intersection between what you're uniquely good at and what your market uniquely needs. That sweet spot becomes the core of your brand positioning.

BUSINESS LESSON: In a crowded marketplace, differentiation isn't optional—it's essential. Define what makes you meaningfully different from everyone else in your space.

BRAND EVOLUTION

Your brand at Rucker wasn't static—it evolved as your game evolved. As you developed new skills, faced new challenges, and entered new stages of your career, your brand adapted while maintaining its core identity.

The same principle applies in business. Your personal brand will and should evolve over time as:

- You develop new skills and expertise
- You identify new market opportunities
- Your industry landscape changes
- Your own goals and interests shift
- You gain new insights about your audience's needs

The key is to evolve intentionally rather than reactively. Strategic brand evolution maintains consistency in your core identity while allowing growth and adaptation to changing circumstances.

I've had to reinvent myself multiple times, especially after basketball. "I went and told myself that I was gonna change my ways and my looks of who I was," I remember deciding. "I felt like if people thought that all they was gonna ever see was, and when they see me, just talk to me about basketball... I'm doing stuff to make you see about my life."

That reinvention wasn't about abandoning my past—it was about building on it, expanding it, taking what worked and applying it to new contexts. The core of who I am remained consistent, but how that core expressed itself evolved.

BUSINESS LESSON: Strong brands evolve strategically while maintaining core identity. Plan your brand evolution rather than letting it happen to you.

FROM PERSONAL BRAND TO BUSINESS BRAND

At Rucker, my personal brand was my business. The name I built opened doors for endorsements, opportunities, and connections. But I've learned that to create something lasting, you need to translate personal brand into business brand—something that can exist beyond your personal presence.

This transition from personal to business brand involves:

- Identifying the elements of your personal brand that can be systematized
- Creating standards and processes that ensure consistent delivery
- Building a team that can embody and extend your brand
- Developing intellectual property that captures your unique approach
- Creating business models that leverage your brand without requiring your constant presence

The goal is to build something that carries your name and embodies your values but doesn't depend entirely on you for its day-to-day execution. This creates scale and longevity that a purely personal brand can't achieve.

BUSINESS LESSON: Build systems that allow your brand to operate beyond your personal capacity. True brand value comes from its ability to scale beyond your direct involvement.

CREATING YOUR PERSONAL BRAND: THE PLAYBOOK

Now it's time to develop your own personal brand. Here's a structured approach to building a brand that creates opportunities and opens doors:

1. **Brand Audit:** Take inventory of how you're currently perceived. Ask people who know you professionally: What three words would you use to describe me? What do you see as my unique strengths? What do you think I'm known for? Their answers may surprise you—and will show you the current state of your brand.

2. **Core Identity Definition:** Based on your authentic strengths and values, define the core elements of your brand:
   - Your unique strengths (what you do exceptionally well)
   - Your values (what you stand for and believe in)
   - Your personality (how you naturally communicate and interact)
   - Your purpose (the impact you want to create)
   - Your audience (who you're ideally positioned to serve)

3. **Differentiation Strategy:** Identify how you're meaningfully different from others in your space. Complete this sentence: "Unlike others who _____, I _____." Make sure your differentiation is relevant to your audience, demonstrable, and difficult to copy.

4. **Brand Expression System:** Develop the tangible elements that express your brand:
   - Visual identity (colors, fonts, imagery that represent you)

- Voice and tone (how you communicate in writing and speaking)
- Key messaging (the core ideas you consistently emphasize)
- Proof points (evidence that supports your brand claims)
- Brand story (the narrative that ties your brand together)

5. **Consistency Plan:** Create systems to ensure your brand is consistently expressed across all touchpoints:
   - Online presence (website, social media, email)
   - In-person interactions (networking, presentations, meetings)
   - Work product (how your brand influences what you deliver)
   - Team alignment (how others who represent you understand your brand)

6. **Reputation Management:** Develop a strategy for building and protecting your reputation:
   - Testimonial gathering (systematically collecting positive feedback)
   - Review monitoring (tracking what's being said about you online)
   - Issue response protocol (how you'll address problems when they arise)
   - Brand ambassador program (activating others to speak on your behalf)

7. **Evolution Framework:** Create a system for intentionally evolving your brand over time:
   - Regular brand review (assessing how well your brand is serving you)

- ○ Market feedback loops (gathering input on how your brand is perceived)
- ○ Competitive positioning review (ensuring continued differentiation)
- ○ Brand innovation process (testing new expressions of your core identity)

Remember, your personal brand isn't just about marketing—it's about alignment between who you are, how you present yourself, and what you deliver. When those elements are in harmony, your brand becomes a powerful asset that creates opportunities even when you're not in the room.

COURT TO BUSINESS: BRAND APPLICATION

On the Court	In Business
Getting a name at Rucker	Establishing your professional reputation
Signature moves and playing style	Your unique approach and methodology
Consistent performance	Reliable delivery of your core promises
Crowd reaction	Customer testimonials and reviews
Media coverage	PR and content marketing
Playing in different tournaments	Expanding your brand to new markets

REAL TALK WITH A-BUTTA

When you have a strong name in the streets, it's easy to think that's enough. I'll be honest—I fell into that trap. I thought that having people yell "Whole Lotta Game!" when I walked in was the end goal. I thought being known by celebrities and having my highlights talked about meant I had made it.

But I learned the hard way that applause doesn't pay bills. Respect in the streets doesn't create generational wealth. A name alone isn't enough.

"We brag about all the people that we connected to and got love for us and respect for us, but we can't take none of that to the bank," I realize now. "I can't go to the bank and say, you know, I did this against Vince Carter, I did that against Stefan Marbury or against Fat Joe."

That realization was humbling. It forced me to think differently about my name—to see it not as an end in itself but as a foundation to build something more lasting. It pushed me to transform street credibility into business credibility, to leverage the connections and reputation I had built for more than just momentary recognition.

The real value of your name—your brand—isn't in how many people know it. It's in what you can do with it. It's in the doors it opens, the opportunities it creates, the platform it provides to build something meaningful.

So yes, build your name. Make it stand for something. Make it recognizable. Make it respected. But don't stop there. Use that name to create something that lasts, something that generates value even when the applause fades, something that can be passed on to the next generation.

Because at the end of the day, your brand isn't just about you. It's about the legacy you leave and the lives you impact along the way.

CHAPTER 5

THE SQUAD - BUILDING YOUR TEAM

"**B**asketball and business mirror each other because when you look at basketball, it's a fraternity and a band of brothers. If you can get with like-minded people, when you play basketball, you become a team, and you can win a lot of things. You can create a lot of good things. And I've learned that in business, if you build with the same kind of like-minded people, you can do the same thing."

In basketball, no matter how talented you are as an individual, you can't win championships alone. Even the greatest players of all time needed a strong team around them—people who complemented their skills, covered their weaknesses, and shared their commitment to winning.

The same principle applies in business. Your success will be determined not just by your individual talents but by the team you build around you. The right squad can multiply your impact, extend your reach, and help you achieve goals that would be impossible on your own.

Building that team isn't about collecting the most impressive resumes or the biggest names. It's about finding the right mix of skills, attitudes, and shared vision that creates something greater than the sum of its parts.

THE LIKE-MINDED PRINCIPLE

One of the most important lessons I've learned about building successful teams comes from reflecting on my basketball experience.

"I looked back in my history and realized that I played with Charles Jones, which was a two-time NCAA scorer. I played with his brother, Lamont Jones, that was like a true natural point guard. And to play with Kareem Reed, another true natural point guard, Stefan Marbury... I didn't realize, until I look back, that I was always playing with people that were like-minded as me, that wanted and knew how to win."

This insight transformed how I think about building teams in business. Like-mindedness doesn't mean everyone thinks exactly the same way— that would create blind spots and limitations. It means sharing core values and a common vision while bringing diverse skills and perspectives.

In business, like-mindedness shows up as:

- Shared values about how to treat people
- Common standards for quality and excellence
- Aligned vision of what you're trying to build
- Similar work ethic and commitment level
- Complementary approaches to problem-solving

When you build a team around these shared foundations, conflicts become productive rather than destructive. Different perspectives strengthen the team rather than dividing it, because they're all oriented toward the same ultimate goals.

BUSINESS LESSON: Build your core team around shared values and vision. Skills can be taught, but alignment on fundamentals is essential.

COMPLEMENTARY STRENGTHS

On the basketball court, a team of all point guards would struggle, no matter how talented each individual player might be. You need different positions, different skill sets, different physical attributes to create a complete team.

Looking back at the teams I played on, I can see how our strengths complemented each other. I had scorers around me. I had facilitators who could distribute the ball. I had defenders who could lock down the opposition. Each of us brought something different that, when combined, created a formidable whole.

In business, this principle of complementary strengths is just as important. A founding team where everyone has the same skills—all visionaries but no executors, all salespeople but no product developers, all creative thinkers but no financial minds—will struggle to build a complete business.

When building your business team, look for people who:

- Excel in areas where you struggle
- Bring perspectives you might not naturally consider
- Have experiences in domains you haven't explored
- Approach problems differently than you do
- Challenge your thinking in productive ways

The goal isn't to surround yourself with people who make you comfortable. It's to build a team where the whole is greater than the sum of its parts.

BUSINESS LESSON: Seek team members with complementary strengths rather than mirror images of yourself. Diversity of skills and perspectives creates completeness.

IDENTIFYING THE RIGHT PLAYERS

In basketball, talent is important, but it's not the only factor in building a winning team. Character, work ethic, basketball IQ, coachability—these intangibles often matter more than raw athletic ability.

The same is true in business. When building your team, you need to look beyond resumes and credentials to the intangible qualities that will determine how someone fits into your organization and contributes to your goals.

Some of the qualities I look for in potential team members include:

- Integrity and trustworthiness
- Growth mindset and willingness to learn
- Resilience in the face of setbacks
- Self-awareness about strengths and weaknesses
- Ability to receive and apply feedback
- Commitment to goals bigger than themselves
- Positive energy that elevates those around them

These qualities can't always be assessed through traditional interviews or background checks. They reveal themselves through deeper conversations, through references from people you trust, through observing how someone handles small challenges before you entrust them with bigger ones.

"When you start to build and connect with like-minded people, that kind of rubs off," I've noticed. "If I knew I was blessed to position myself to be around those kind of people on the basketball court, that's the same kind of motivation you got to have off the court. You have to position yourself around people that's doing good."

BUSINESS LESSON: Assess character and cultural fit as carefully as skills and experience. The right intangibles often predict success better than the right resume.

CREATING TEAM CHEMISTRY

Having talented individuals doesn't automatically create a great team. I've seen squads with incredible individual players fail because they couldn't function effectively together. Team chemistry—that special alchemy that happens when individuals truly connect and align—can't be forced, but it can be cultivated.

In my experience, team chemistry develops when:

- There's genuine respect for each individual's contribution
- Communication is open, honest, and constructive
- Everyone understands both their role and the bigger picture
- Success is celebrated collectively, not individually
- Challenges are faced together rather than blamed on individuals
- Trust allows people to focus on their strengths rather than covering their weaknesses

As a leader, you can't manufacture chemistry, but you can create conditions where it's more likely to develop. You can model the behaviors you want to see. You can create opportunities for team members to connect on a human level, not just a professional one. You can address issues that undermine trust before they become toxic.

"That energy is contagious," I've found. "The help is what really helps us. Being around the help. You become the help."

BUSINESS LESSON: Team chemistry creates competitive advantage. Invest in building connections between team members, not just adding individual talent.

CLARITY OF ROLES

On a basketball team, everyone needs to understand their role. The point guard knows they're responsible for running the offense. The center knows they need to protect the rim. The shooting guard knows they're counted on for perimeter scoring. When roles are clear, everyone can focus on excelling in their area rather than trying to do everything.

In business teams, this same role clarity is essential. Each person needs to understand:

- Their specific responsibilities
- How their role connects to the larger mission
- Where their authority begins and ends
- Who they can turn to for different types of support
- How their performance will be measured
- How their work impacts others on the team

Without this clarity, teams waste energy through duplication of effort, dropped balls, and unnecessary conflicts. With it, each person can focus on maximizing their contribution in their specific area.

Role clarity doesn't mean rigid boundaries that never change. As teams evolve and individuals develop, roles should adapt accordingly. But even as roles evolve, the clarity about what's expected at any given time remains important.

BUSINESS LESSON: Define roles clearly while allowing for evolution. When everyone knows what they're responsible for, the team operates more efficiently and effectively.

THE RIGHT PEOPLE IN THE RIGHT POSITIONS

One of the insights I've gained from both basketball and business is the importance of positioning people according to their natural strengths rather than trying to force them into roles that don't fit them.

"You gotta kind of keep people in the field of what, where they're at and what they're good at," I explain. "I try not to bring Danny Green involved into anything that I know Joe Kim Noah might be good at because he's more of a world Ambassador when it comes to outside of America versus what's going on inside of America."

This principle applies to business teams as well. When you position people in roles that align with their natural strengths and passions, you get their best work with the least friction. When you force people into roles that fight against their nature, you get mediocre results and unnecessary struggle.

This doesn't mean people can't grow and develop in new areas. But that growth should build on natural strengths rather than trying to create qualities that simply aren't there.

"If you can keep people in a space where their love for the character who they are, nine times out of 10, that business or collaboration will work out," I've found. "You don't want people to be used for photo ops when you know you can strategically put people in a position where they already have a love for something."

BUSINESS LESSON: Position team members where their natural strengths can shine. Role alignment creates better results with less effort and more satisfaction.

BUILDING A CULTURE OF GROWTH

The best basketball teams aren't just collections of talented individuals— they're environments where everyone is constantly improving. Players push each other, coaches develop talent, and the overall level of play elevates over time.

In business, this culture of growth is equally important. Your team shouldn't just execute today's plan—it should be developing the capabilities to tackle tomorrow's challenges. This happens when you create an environment where:

- Learning is valued as much as performance
- Mistakes are treated as opportunities for growth rather than reasons for punishment
- Feedback flows freely in all directions

- Individual development is seen as a team investment
- Success is defined not just by results but by improvement
- Innovation and experimentation are encouraged

Building this culture starts with your own example as a leader. If you demonstrate a commitment to your own growth, admit your mistakes, seek feedback, and continuously improve, others will follow that lead.

BUSINESS LESSON: Create a culture where growth is expected and supported. Teams that improve together can tackle increasingly complex challenges over time.

LEADERSHIP THAT SERVES

In basketball, the best leaders aren't always the ones who score the most points or get the most attention. They're the ones who make everyone around them better, who put the team's success above individual accolades, who lead by example and lift others up.

I've tried to bring this same approach to leadership in business and life. "Being happy and having that happy energy and having that motivated energy, I think energy is underrated," I reflect. "I think that in order for you to get others to feel like it's worth them taking a chance and being able to build with you, you got to have a certain type of energy."

Leadership isn't about demanding respect or asserting authority. It's about creating conditions where others can succeed, where they feel valued and motivated, where they want to bring their best because they believe in what you're building together.

Some of the leadership principles I've found most effective include:

- Leading by example rather than directive
- Giving credit generously while taking responsibility
- Providing both challenge and support
- Listening deeply before speaking
- Being transparent about both successes and failures
- Prioritizing the team's growth over personal recognition

"I get more light from helping others, which then trickles down to me," I've discovered. "I stay grounded because I'm able to keep you in your light."

BUSINESS LESSON: True leadership serves the team's growth and success. When you elevate others, the entire enterprise rises.

BUILDING YOUR BUSINESS TEAM: THE PLAYBOOK

Now it's time to build your own winning team. Here's a structured approach to assembling a squad that can help you achieve your business goals:

1. **Team Needs Assessment:** Identify the key functions and capabilities your business requires. Be honest about your own strengths and the gaps that need to be filled. Create a priority list of the most critical roles to fill first.

2. **Values and Culture Definition:** Before hiring anyone, clearly articulate the values and culture you want to build. Document these so they can be shared with potential team members and used as evaluation criteria.

3. **Role Design:** For each position you need to fill, create a clear role description that includes:
   - o Primary responsibilities
   - o Required skills and experience
   - o Character qualities and cultural attributes
   - o How success will be measured
   - o Growth paths within the organization

4. **Sourcing Strategy:** Develop a plan for finding potential team members that goes beyond posting job listings. Consider:
   - o Your existing network (but be careful about hiring friends without proper vetting)
   - o Industry events and communities
   - o Educational institutions
   - o Referrals from trusted connections
   - o Social media and professional networks

5. **Evaluation Process:** Create a structured approach to assessing candidates that includes:
   - o Initial screening for basic qualifications
   - o Skills assessment relevant to actual job duties
   - o Cultural fit interviews with multiple team members
   - o Reference checks with specific questions about work style and character
   - o Trial projects where possible to see how candidates actually perform

6. **Onboarding System:** Design a process to integrate new team members effectively:
   - o Clear explanation of values, expectations, and norms
   - o Connection to the larger vision and how their role contributes
   - o Early wins to build confidence and momentum

- Regular check-ins during the initial period
- Mentorship or buddy system for ongoing support

7. **Team Development Plan:** Create a strategy for helping your team grow together:
   - Regular team building activities (both work-related and social)
   - Open communication channels for feedback and ideas
   - Recognition systems that celebrate both individual and team achievements
   - Conflict resolution protocols for addressing issues constructively
   - Continuous learning opportunities for skill development

Remember, building a great team takes time. It's better to move deliberately and find the right people than to fill positions quickly with people who aren't truly aligned with your vision and values.

COURT TO BUSINESS: TEAM APPLICATION

On the Court	In Business
Player positions and roles	Organizational structure and role definition
Team practice and drills	Team training and skill development
Game strategy and playbook	Business strategy and operating procedures
Locker room culture	Organizational culture and values
Coach and captain leadership	Executive and management approach
In-game adjustments	Adaptability to market changes

REAL TALK WITH A-BUTTA

When I look at the teams that have been most successful—both in basketball and in business—I notice something important: They don't just work together. They grow together.

The best teams I played on weren't just collections of talent. They were groups that challenged each other, supported each other, and ultimately elevated each other. We made each other better through our connections, our communication, and our shared commitment to excellence.

In building business teams, I'm looking for that same dynamic. I want to surround myself with people who aren't just skilled at what they do, but who are committed to growth—their own and others'. People who understand that rising tides lift all boats, that success is sweeter when it's shared, that the strongest teams win not despite their differences but because of them.

"I'll never forget Cameron teaching me to make sure that you always reinventing yourself," I acknowledge. "Always stand for something before for anything."

That's the kind of wisdom that gets passed through teams—the lessons that go beyond skills to shape character and mindset. It's why who you build with matters as much as what you're building.

So as you assemble your squad, look beyond the immediate needs of your business. Look for people who will not just fill roles but grow into them and beyond them. Look for people who will challenge you to be better while supporting you when you stumble. Look for people who share your vision but bring their own unique perspective on how to achieve it.

Because at the end of the day, business isn't just about transactions. It's about transformation—of markets, of customers, of communities, and most importantly, of the people who make up your team. When you build the right squad, everyone wins.

CHAPTER 6

THE HUSTLE - EXECUTION AND WORK ETHIC

"I *was always kind of like a gym rat. My coach gave me the key to the gym, and I'd be there when nobody else was. What people saw was the game-winning shot. What they didn't see was the thousand shots before that, when the gym was empty and nobody was watching. That's the hustle—putting in work when there's no applause, no recognition, just you and your goals."*

In basketball, they call it hustle—that relentless energy that has you diving for loose balls, fighting through screens, sprinting back on defense, and going after rebounds against taller opponents. Hustle isn't about talent or skill. It's about effort, determination, and the willingness to do whatever it takes to win.

In business, hustle is just as important. It's the execution engine that turns vision into reality, that transforms plans into results, that separates dreamers from doers. Without hustle, the greatest ideas remain just that—ideas, unfulfilled and unrealized.

But true hustle isn't just about working hard. It's about working smart, working consistently, and working with purpose. It's about bringing energy and intensity to the things that truly matter while eliminating what doesn't.

THE EARLY ADVANTAGE

One of the most important lessons I learned from my coaches was about the power of being early: "Early is on time, on time is late, late is unacceptable."

At first, I didn't understand. If practice was at three o'clock, why did I need to be there at 2:30 or 2:45? But over time, I realized what they were really teaching me—those who show up early get advantages others don't:

- Extra time to prepare mentally and physically
- One-on-one attention from coaches
- Space to work on specific skills without distraction
- The habit of exceeding expectations, not just meeting them
- The reputation for reliability that opens doors later

In business, this same principle applies. The entrepreneurs who arrive early to market trends, who prepare more thoroughly for opportunities, who exceed deadlines rather than barely meeting them—these are the ones who create advantages for themselves.

Being early isn't just about time—it's about mindset. It's about positioning yourself ahead of expectations rather than scrambling to catch up to them. It's about creating margin that allows you to be thoughtful and strategic rather than reactive and rushed.

BUSINESS LESSON: Position yourself ahead of expectations. The space between early and on-time is where preparation creates opportunity.

PREPARATION PREVENTS PROBLEMS

My mindset toward preparation was simple but powerful: "Failing to prepare is preparing to fail."

On the court, preparation took many forms—studying opponents' tendencies, practicing specific situations that might arise in games, conditioning my body to handle the physical demands, mentally rehearsing scenarios so I could respond without hesitation.

This discipline of preparation translated directly to business. When I approach opportunities now, I think about preparation in terms of:

- Research that informs decisions
- Contingency planning for potential obstacles
- Practice runs before important presentations or meetings
- Building systems that support consistent execution
- Creating buffers for unexpected challenges

Preparation isn't about eliminating all uncertainty—that's impossible in both basketball and business. It's about reducing unnecessary uncertainty so you can focus your energy and creativity on the challenges that couldn't be anticipated.

"If you're not structuring and you're not preparing, you're kind of setting yourself up to get ready to deal with loose ends," I've found. "The more that you constantly sharpen your skills, the better you'll be able to handle whatever comes your way."

BUSINESS LESSON: Thorough preparation eliminates preventable problems. Invest time upfront to save time, energy, and reputation later.

CONSISTENT EXECUTION

In basketball, game-winning shots get the highlights, but championships are won through consistent execution of fundamentals over time. The players who show up day after day, who maintain their intensity through practice and games, who execute the game plan even when they're tired or things aren't going well—these are the players coaches trust in crucial moments.

The same principle applies in business. Success rarely comes from a single brilliant moment or decision. It comes from consistent execution of key activities over time:

- Delivering on promises to customers
- Maintaining quality standards even when it's difficult
- Following through on commitments to team members
- Persisting with marketing efforts even when results aren't immediate
- Making incremental improvements to products and processes

This consistency isn't glamorous. It doesn't make headlines. But it's the foundation upon which lasting success is built. It's what transforms occasional brilliance into sustained excellence.

"Success doesn't happen overnight," I remind people. "You have to understand the journey and the process, and within the journey and the process, you should be learning structure."

BUSINESS LESSON: Consistent execution of fundamentals creates compounding success. Trust the process even when results aren't immediately visible.

ENERGY MANAGEMENT

Hustle requires energy—physical, mental, and emotional. But many entrepreneurs make the mistake of confusing activity with productivity, of working hard but not necessarily on the right things, of burning themselves out because they haven't learned to manage their energy effectively.

In basketball, I learned that intensity needs to be balanced with recovery, that effort needs to be focused on high-impact activities, that energy needs to be managed across a long season rather than burned all at once.

These same principles apply to business hustle:

- Identify the high-leverage activities that create disproportionate results, and focus your best energy there
- Create rhythms of intense work and meaningful recovery
- Eliminate or delegate low-value tasks that drain energy without creating significant returns
- Recognize your personal energy patterns and schedule important work for your peak times
- Fuel your body and mind properly through nutrition, sleep, and mental breaks

"Being happy and having that happy energy and having that motivated energy, I think energy is underrated," I've observed. "In order for you to get others to feel like it's worth them taking a chance and being able to build with you, you got to have a certain type of energy."

BUSINESS LESSON: Manage your energy as carefully as your time. Sustainable hustle comes from working intensely on the right things, not from working constantly on everything.

THE DISCIPLINE OF FOCUS

One of the most valuable lessons I learned through basketball was the discipline of focus—the ability to direct my attention and effort toward what matters most, even amid distractions and competing priorities.

On the court, focus meant staying present in the moment, executing the current play rather than dwelling on the last one or worrying about the next one. It meant tuning out the crowd noise and the trash talk to concentrate on what I could control.

In business, this same discipline is crucial for effective execution. It shows up as:

- Identifying the few critical priorities that will move your business forward, and saying no to everything else
- Breaking large goals into specific, actionable tasks that can be completed one by one
- Creating environments that minimize distractions during deep work
- Building daily routines that protect your focus and direct it toward high-value activities
- Measuring what matters so your attention stays on real progress, not just busy work

"When I got an opportunity to get away from New York City and went to Milford Academy up in Connecticut, I just had the gym. I had the key to the gym all the time, and I think that was a major key for me—isolation.

My isolation helped me get stronger. Helped me focus on getting better, and I didn't really have no distractions."

This kind of focused isolation—whether physical or just mental—creates space for the deep work that moves you forward. It allows you to develop skills and create value in ways that constant distraction never will.

BUSINESS LESSON: Cultivate the discipline of focus. Your ability to concentrate deeply on high-value work will separate you from those who are constantly reactive and distracted.

THE DAILY GRIND

Championships aren't won on game day—they're won in the countless practices leading up to it. Businesses aren't built through occasional brilliant moves—they're built through the daily grind of showing up, putting in work, and making incremental progress.

What separates successful entrepreneurs from unsuccessful ones often isn't their ideas, their funding, or even their skills. It's their ability to embrace the daily grind—to find meaning and motivation in the mundane tasks that, accumulated over time, create extraordinary results.

The daily grind includes:

- Routine tasks that maintain operations
- Regular check-ins with team members and customers
- Ongoing learning and skill development
- Consistent marketing and sales activities
- Performance review and process improvement

None of these activities is particularly exciting on its own. But together, performed consistently over time, they create the foundation for breakthrough results.

The key to embracing the daily grind is connecting it to your larger purpose. When you understand how today's small tasks contribute to tomorrow's big goals, they take on new meaning and energy.

BUSINESS LESSON: Embrace the daily grind as the path to extraordinary results. Find meaning in the mundane by connecting it to your larger purpose.

ACCOUNTABILITY SYSTEMS

In basketball, accountability comes from many sources—coaches who track performance metrics, teammates who expect your best effort, fans who respond to your play. These external accountability structures help maintain focus and intensity even when internal motivation fluctuates.

In business, especially when you're building something new, these external accountability structures may not exist naturally. You need to create them:

- Strategic partners who expect deliverables
- Advisors or mentors who review your progress
- Public commitments that create expectations
- Tracking systems that make performance visible
- Team members who count on consistent execution

Without these accountability systems, it's easy for hustle to fade when challenges arise or motivation dips. With them, you create external reinforcement for the internal commitment to execution.

"The more and more that you constantly is structuring yourself in your business... structuring yourself and structuring your business eventually turns into success," I've found.

BUSINESS LESSON: Build systems of accountability that support consistent execution. External structures reinforce internal commitment when motivation naturally fluctuates.

EXECUTING YOUR BUSINESS VISION: THE PLAYBOOK

Now it's time to turn your vision into reality through consistent execution. Here's a structured approach to bringing the hustle that transforms plans into results:

1. **Priority Identification:** Determine the 3-5 key activities that will create the most significant progress toward your goals. Be ruthlessly selective—not everything that seems important actually is. Ask: If I could only focus on a few things, which would move the needle most?

2. **Daily Execution System:** Create a daily routine that ensures consistent action on your priorities:
   o Morning planning ritual to set daily targets
   o Time blocking for focused work on high-priority activities
   o Regular breaks for energy management

- End-of-day review to celebrate wins and prepare for tomorrow
- Weekly reset to maintain alignment with larger goals

3. **Productivity Environment:** Design your physical and digital workspace to support focused execution:
    - Minimize distractions during deep work periods
    - Create visual reminders of priorities and progress
    - Establish clear boundaries between work and personal time
    - Optimize tools and technology for efficiency
    - Surround yourself with people who elevate your standards

4. **Measurement Framework:** Develop simple metrics to track your execution and results:
    - Input metrics (activities you control)
    - Output metrics (results those activities produce)
    - Leading indicators (early signs of progress)
    - Lagging indicators (ultimate outcomes)
    - Qualitative feedback (subjective assessments)

5. **Accountability Structures:** Build systems that hold you to your commitments:
    - Accountability partners who check in regularly
    - Public commitments that create social pressure
    - Financial incentives tied to execution
    - Team dependencies that require your follow-through
    - Regular review sessions with advisors or mentors

6. **Energy Management Plan:** Create strategies to sustain your hustle over the long term:
    - Identify your personal energy patterns and leverage them
    - Build recovery periods into your schedule
    - Eliminate energy drains that don't contribute to results

- o Develop pre-performance routines that optimize your state
- o Create celebration rituals that acknowledge progress

7. **Continuous Improvement Process:** Establish a system for refining your execution over time:
   - o Weekly review of what worked and what didn't
   - o Monthly adjustment of priorities and strategies
   - o Quarterly deeper assessment of direction and approach
   - o Annual reset of vision and long-term goals
   - o Ongoing skill development in areas that limit your execution

Remember, execution isn't about perfection—it's about progress. The goal isn't to execute flawlessly every day but to maintain momentum through consistent action, learning, and adjustment.

COURT TO BUSINESS: HUSTLE APPLICATION

On the Court	In Business
Practice routines and drills	Daily productivity systems
Game preparation	Market and opportunity research
Playing through fatigue	Persisting through challenging periods
Diving for loose balls	Going above and beyond for customers
Extra shooting after practice	Continuous skill development
Film study and adjustment	Performance review and improvement

REAL TALK WITH A-BUTTA

I started my podcast in 2016 and didn't get sponsorship until 2024. That's eight years of showing up, creating content, building relationships, and believing in the vision when there was little external validation.

"Getting into a lane and doing something not really knowing, in this entrepreneurship world versus really getting a job and having a 401(k), to really think about a retirement knowing you got kids—these choices ain't easy," I admit.

But the determination I always had on the court is the same mindset I brought to business. I've always told myself that if I became a legend on the court, there's no way I couldn't become one off the court.

That belief has kept me going when results weren't immediate, when doors didn't open as quickly as I hoped, when the path forward wasn't always clear. It's kept me putting in work day after day, building slowly but steadily toward the vision.

That's what real hustle is about—not the flashy, social media version that's all about the grind but no substance. Real hustle is showing up consistently even when no one is watching. It's doing the unglamorous work that creates the foundation for everything else. It's trusting the process even when the results aren't yet visible.

"The determination that I've always had on the court is the same mindset that I have off the court," I explain to those coming up behind me.

If there's one thing I want you to take from this chapter, it's this: Execution isn't optional. The greatest vision, the most talented team, the strongest brand—none of it matters without the hustle to bring it to life. Decide what matters most, build systems to support consistent action, and then put in the work day after day after day.

That's how legends are built, on the court and in business.

CHAPTER 7

THE DEFENSE - PROTECTING WHAT YOU'VE BUILT

"In basketball, everybody wants to talk about offense—the crossovers, the dunks, the three-pointers. But championships are won with defense. The same is true in business. It's not just about building something great—it's about protecting it, strengthening it, and making sure it can withstand the challenges that will come."

Defense in basketball doesn't get the highlights or the glory. You rarely see SportsCenter leading with a perfect defensive rotation or a well-executed box-out. But ask any championship coach, and they'll tell you—defense wins championships.

In business, the same principle applies. Building a successful enterprise isn't just about growth, innovation, and offense. It's also about protection, risk management, and defense. The businesses that last aren't just the ones that grow the fastest—they're the ones that build strong foundations that can weather storms and sustain success over time.

This chapter is about how to defend what you've built—your business, your brand, your reputation, your legacy. Because getting to the top is one challenge; staying there is another entirely.

PROTECTING YOUR REPUTATION

At Rucker, your reputation was everything. It determined whether teams wanted you, whether the crowd respected you, whether opportunities came your way. And reputations that took years to build could be damaged in moments if you didn't protect them carefully.

"I kind of had to learn the hard way, which was, I don't get props for standing on other people that stood on their own," I reflect. "I had to learn who I was, and once I learned who I was, I'm passing it off to someone else to find out who you are, because if you don't find out who you are, you might block yourself from some spaces and from places that you belong in."

In business, your reputation is equally valuable and equally vulnerable. It's built through consistent delivery on promises, through ethical handling of challenges, through authentic relationships with customers and partners. And like on the court, it can be damaged quickly if not protected.

Some key strategies for protecting your business reputation include:

- Delivering consistently on the promises you make to customers
- Being transparent about mistakes and addressing them promptly
- Establishing clear values and ensuring every team member understands and embodies them

- Monitoring what's being said about your brand online and responding appropriately
- Building strong relationships with key stakeholders before challenges arise

"Now that I'm more conscious of looking at what I'm choosing to do, it speaks a little bit more on my character and who I'm becoming," I explain. This awareness is the first step in reputation management—recognizing that every action, every interaction, every decision either strengthens or weakens how you're perceived.

BUSINESS LESSON: Your reputation is one of your most valuable business assets. Protect it through intentional actions and consistent alignment with your values.

FINANCIAL DEFENSE

In basketball, defensive fundamentals include proper stance, positioning, awareness, and communication. In business, financial defense has its own fundamentals that protect your enterprise from vulnerabilities.

Many entrepreneurs focus exclusively on revenue and growth while neglecting the defensive financial practices that ensure sustainability. They build businesses that look impressive on the outside but lack the structural integrity to withstand challenges.

Strong financial defense includes:

- Maintaining adequate cash reserves for unexpected challenges
- Understanding your margins and protecting them from erosion

- Diversifying revenue streams to reduce dependency on any single source
- Creating clear financial controls and review processes
- Building sustainable growth rather than chasing vanity metrics
- Investing in insurance and risk management appropriate to your business

Just as a team with weak defensive fundamentals will eventually be exposed, a business without strong financial practices will eventually face challenges it can't overcome. The time to build these practices isn't during a crisis—it's before one arrives.

"If you're not structuring and you're not preparing, you're kind of setting yourself up to get ready to deal with loose ends," I warn. This applies especially to financial structure and preparation.

BUSINESS LESSON: Build strong financial fundamentals even when business is good. Defensive financial practices create resilience when challenges inevitably arise.

LEGAL PROTECTION

On the court, rules provide structure and protection. In business, legal frameworks serve the same purpose—they define boundaries, establish consequences, and protect what you've built from those who might exploit or damage it.

Many entrepreneurs, especially those from communities like mine, neglect legal protection until problems arise. But by then, it's often too late to establish the defenses that could have prevented or minimized the damage.

Key areas of legal protection for your business include:

- Proper business structure (LLC, corporation, etc.) that limits personal liability
- Clear contracts with customers, suppliers, partners, and team members
- Intellectual property protection for your brand, content, and innovations
- Compliance with regulations relevant to your industry
- Privacy and data protection practices that meet legal requirements
- Dispute resolution procedures that address issues before they escalate

These legal protections aren't just about avoiding problems—they're about creating the foundation for confident growth. When you know your business is properly protected, you can focus your energy on creation and expansion rather than worry and damage control.

BUSINESS LESSON: Invest in appropriate legal protection before problems arise. Legal defense creates the security to focus on offense.

RELATIONSHIP DEFENSE

In basketball, team defense is always stronger than individual defense. Players who communicate effectively, who help each other, who move as a coordinated unit—they create a defensive force that's hard to break down.

In business, your network of relationships provides similar defensive strength. Strong connections with customers, partners, suppliers, team members, and community create a support system that can help you weather challenges and recover from setbacks.

Building defensive relationships means:

- Creating genuine connections beyond transactions
- Demonstrating loyalty and support before asking for it in return
- Communicating openly and honestly, especially during difficulties
- Recognizing and acknowledging the contributions of others
- Being the kind of partner you would want during challenging times

"You always know who you are when you build with the right people," I've learned. "With God's children, they see a little bit above mistakes. I'm positioning myself in that way as well, to make myself see that I've made mistakes, but I've been forgiven."

This approach to relationships—seeing beyond mistakes, focusing on growth, supporting each other through challenges—creates a network that defends you when you're vulnerable and helps you recover when you stumble.

BUSINESS LESSON: Strong authentic relationships create defensive resilience. Invest in building genuine connections before you need their support.

COMPETITIVE DEFENSE

On the basketball court, defensive strategy includes understanding opponents' tendencies, taking away their preferred options, and forcing them into lower-percentage plays. In business, competitive defense follows similar principles.

Effective competitive defense isn't about obsessing over competitors or trying to copy everything they do. It's about understanding the competitive landscape well enough to:

- Identify and protect your unique advantages
- Recognize emerging threats before they become critical
- Anticipate competitive moves and prepare appropriate responses
- Monitor market shifts that could change competitive dynamics
- Build barriers to entry that protect your position

"I try to make sure that I'm on time, and when I say on time, meaning that you have to prepare," I emphasize. "If you're not preparing, you're kind of setting yourself up to get ready to deal with what I call loose ends."

In competitive terms, those "loose ends" are the vulnerabilities that competitors can exploit if you haven't prepared properly. Competitive defense is about identifying and addressing those vulnerabilities before others can take advantage of them.

BUSINESS LESSON: Understand your competitive position and protect it strategically. Anticipate threats rather than just reacting to them.

TECHNOLOGICAL DEFENSE

In today's business environment, technology presents both opportunities and vulnerabilities. The entrepreneurs who neglect technological defense leave themselves exposed to risks that can threaten everything they've built.

Technological defense includes:

- Cybersecurity practices appropriate to your business
- Data backup and recovery systems that prevent catastrophic loss
- Privacy protections that safeguard customer and business information
- Authentication and access controls that prevent unauthorized use
- Regular updates and maintenance of critical systems
- Contingency plans for technology failures or breaches

For many small business owners, especially those from communities with limited technological resources, these defensive practices may seem overwhelming or unnecessary. But in today's interconnected world, technological vulnerabilities can affect businesses of any size in any industry.

The level of technological defense you need depends on your specific business, but the principle remains the same—identify what's most important to protect and build appropriate safeguards around it.

BUSINESS LESSON: Build technological defenses appropriate to your business risks. In today's digital environment, technological vulnerabilities can threaten your entire enterprise.

CREATING YOUR BUSINESS DEFENSE SYSTEM: THE PLAYBOOK

Now it's time to build your own defensive system to protect what you've created. Here's a structured approach to identifying and addressing vulnerabilities before they become problems:

1. **Vulnerability Audit:** Assess your business across key defensive categories:
    o   Reputation risks (what could damage how you're perceived)
    o   Financial vulnerabilities (what could threaten financial stability)
    o   Legal exposures (where you lack appropriate protection)
    o   Relationship weaknesses (where critical connections need strengthening)
    o   Competitive threats (where others could undermine your position)
    o   Technological risks (where systems or data are vulnerable)

2. **Risk Prioritization:** For each vulnerability identified, assess:
    o   Potential impact if the risk materializes
    o   Probability of the risk occurring
    o   Your current level of protection
    o   Cost and complexity of improving protection
    o   Use this assessment to prioritize where to focus defensive efforts

3. **Protection Plan:** For your highest-priority vulnerabilities, develop specific protective measures:

- Preventive controls (reducing the likelihood of problems)
- Detective controls (identifying issues quickly when they occur)
- Corrective controls (minimizing damage and facilitating recovery)
- Insurance and risk transfer (shifting some risk to others)

4. **Response Protocols:** Create plans for how you'll respond if key risks materialize:
   - Initial response steps and responsibilities
   - Communication strategies for different stakeholders
   - Resource allocation during crisis situations
   - Recovery and return to normal operations
   - Learning and improvement after incidents

5. **Regular Review System:** Establish a process for ongoing defensive maintenance:
   - Quarterly review of key risks and protective measures
   - Annual comprehensive defense audit
   - Specific triggers that prompt immediate reassessment
   - Continuous improvement of defensive systems

6. **Team Alignment:** Ensure everyone involved in your business understands:
   - Their role in protecting key assets
   - Warning signs they should watch for
   - How to report concerns or incidents
   - Their responsibilities during response situations

7. **Defensive Culture:** Build defense into your organizational mindset:
   - Celebrate prevention as much as achievement
   - Recognize and reward protective behaviors

    ○   Create psychological safety for raising concerns

    ○   Model defensive thinking in leadership discussions

Remember, the goal of business defense isn't to become risk-averse or paranoid. It's to create the security and stability that allow you to take appropriate offensive risks with confidence. When you know your foundation is solid, you can build higher without fear of collapse.

COURT TO BUSINESS: DEFENSE APPLICATION

On the Court	In Business
Defensive stance and positioning	Proactive risk management
Help defense and rotation	Team awareness of vulnerabilities
Shot blocking and rim protection	Legal and contractual safeguards
Defensive communication	Transparent risk discussion
Anticipating offensive moves	Competitive intelligence and preparation
Defensive rebounds	Recovering from setbacks

REAL TALK WITH A-BUTTA

One of the hardest lessons I've had to learn is that defense isn't just about protecting against external threats—sometimes it's about protecting yourself from your own tendencies and patterns.

"I kind of fell victim to that character, that attitude," I admit when reflecting on how my approach sometimes kept me out of rooms I should have been in. "That's the reason why we kept out of rooms, and our character and our attitude is going to be the reason whether we're in the room or we're out."

This is the most personal form of business defense—recognizing and addressing the habits, mindsets, and behaviors that undermine your own success. For me, it was adopting an attitude that didn't align with who I really was. For you, it might be different—perhaps overcommitting, avoiding necessary confrontation, perfectionism that prevents completion, or difficulty delegating.

Whatever your personal vulnerabilities, defending against them requires the same approach as defending against external threats: honest assessment, prioritization, and deliberate action to strengthen weak areas.

This isn't about being hard on yourself or dwelling on flaws. It's about the same clear-eyed assessment that great athletes apply to their game. They don't take it personally when a coach points out defensive weaknesses—they get to work addressing them.

"I try not to run anymore from adversity," I share. "I'm a cancer. I'm a crab. So I might go in my shell, but I've learned that I also have claws, and I can clap back, I can protect myself."

That's the balance that effective defense requires—not running from challenges, but not being naive about them either. Recognizing vulnerabilities while believing in your ability to address them. Preparing for difficulties while maintaining faith in your vision.

Because ultimately, the purpose of defense isn't just preservation—it's providing the foundation for greater achievement. When what you've built is secure, you can focus your energy on creating rather than repairing, on advancing rather than recovering, on offense rather than just defense.

And that's when you truly begin to win the game.

CHAPTER 8

THE COMEBACK - OVERCOMING ADVERSITY

*"*After I turned 33 and took my first loss in one-on-one in basketball, most people don't know this, I've never lost a one-on-one until publicly, the world saw me lose to Jesse Sapp. And after I lost to Jesse Sapp, I had to reinvent myself. I went and told myself that I was gonna change my ways and my looks of who I was. I had to figure out how to reinvent myself in a way where I could show you that life after basketball can still be successful, just like it was for me on the basketball court.*"*

In basketball, the most memorable games aren't the blowouts—they're the comebacks. Those moments when a team is down, seemingly defeated, but finds a way to dig deep, adjust their approach, and turn things around. These comeback victories reveal character in a way that easy wins never can.

In business and life, adversity is equally revealing. It's not the success that comes easily that defines you—it's how you respond when things get hard, when you face setbacks, when you have to reinvent yourself in the face of changing circumstances.

This chapter is about the comeback—how to face adversity, how to adapt when your original plan doesn't work out, how to reinvent yourself when necessary, and how to build the resilience that turns setbacks into setups for greater success.

THE INEVITABILITY OF ADVERSITY

In basketball, no matter how talented you are, how well you prepare, or how hard you work, adversity is inevitable. You'll face injuries, tough losses, shooting slumps, and moments of doubt. No player, not even the greatest of all time, escapes these challenges.

The same reality exists in business. No matter how strong your vision, how solid your team, how excellent your execution, you will face adversity:

- Market conditions will change unexpectedly
- Competitors will emerge with new approaches
- Key team members will leave at critical moments
- Products that seemed promising will underperform
- External events will disrupt your plans
- Personal challenges will impact your business

The question isn't whether you'll face adversity—it's how you'll respond when it arrives. Will you be caught unprepared, paralyzed by surprise and disappointment? Or will you recognize adversity as an inevitable part of the journey and be ready to navigate through it?

"I think a lot of people with mental health, a lot of people dwell a lot on the stabbing in the back, or the mistakes, or the falling and stuff," I observe. "But when you talk about God, he teaches you that a lot of these mishaps, a lot of these, what do you call it, going through the furnace, through the fire, is shaping the diamonds."

This perspective doesn't make adversity easy, but it makes it meaningful. It transforms obstacles from random bad luck into purposeful challenges that shape you into something stronger and more valuable than you were before.

BUSINESS LESSON: Accept adversity as inevitable rather than exceptional. This mental shift allows you to prepare for challenges rather than being surprised by them.

THE REINVENTION MINDSET

One of the most important lessons I've learned through both basketball and business is the power of reinvention—the ability to evolve your approach, your skills, your identity when circumstances demand it.

"You gotta constantly reinvent yourself," Cameron taught me, and it's advice I'll never forget. "Stand for something before for anything."

This reinvention mindset is crucial for navigating adversity. It allows you to see setbacks not as the end of your story but as the beginning of a new chapter. It helps you recognize when one approach isn't working and find the courage to try another. It gives you permission to evolve while still staying true to your core values.

In business, reinvention might mean:

- Pivoting your product to address a different market need
- Developing new skills to remain relevant in changing conditions

- Adjusting your business model to reflect new market realities
- Rebranding to connect with different customer segments
- Restructuring your organization to increase efficiency or effectiveness

The entrepreneurs who thrive long-term aren't necessarily those with the best initial ideas—they're those most willing and able to reinvent themselves as conditions change.

BUSINESS LESSON: Cultivate a reinvention mindset that sees change as opportunity rather than threat. The ability to evolve is often the difference between businesses that survive and those that thrive.

FACING FAILURE PRODUCTIVELY

In basketball, every player misses shots. Even the greatest shooters of all time miss about half their attempts. But what separates great players from average ones isn't their success rate—it's how they respond to misses. Do they let one missed shot affect the next? Do they stop shooting altogether? Or do they learn, adjust, and confidently take the next shot?

In business, failure is equally common and equally informative. Products fail. Marketing campaigns underperform. Hires don't work out. Partnerships dissolve. The question isn't whether you'll experience failure—it's how you'll process it when you do.

Productive responses to failure include:

- Analyzing what happened without excessive self-blame

- Extracting specific lessons that can improve future attempts
- Separating the failure of an approach from your identity as a person
- Maintaining perspective on the relative importance of the setback
- Reengaging quickly rather than withdrawing in shame

"I'm grateful for some of the people that I grew up with and was around, because they always taught me that you gotta constantly reinvent yourself," I reflect. This support system helped me face failures not as final verdicts but as feedback that informed my next move.

BUSINESS LESSON: Develop a productive relationship with failure that extracts lessons without extracting confidence. How you process setbacks often determines whether they become stepping stones or stumbling blocks.

THE ADVERSITY ADVANTAGE

While nobody seeks out adversity, those who navigate it successfully often discover that it creates advantages that wouldn't have developed otherwise:

- Resilience that allows you to withstand future challenges
- Creativity born from the necessity to find new approaches
- Deeper appreciation for success when it arrives
- Authenticity that comes from being tested and proven
- Wisdom that can only be gained through experience
- Stories that connect powerfully with others facing similar challenges

I've experienced this adversity advantage firsthand. "I credit a lot to isola-tion," I share. "Isolation really helps you evolve and be able to get better in anything in life. And a lot of us, we don't like to isolate, don't like to be alone. But sometimes the aloneness gives you a chance to put some pieces back together and come back even stronger."

That period of isolation—which felt like adversity at the time—created space for growth and development that wouldn't have happened other-wise. It allowed me to level up my game in ways that surprised people when I returned.

In business, the same dynamic often plays out. The companies that sur-vive significant challenges frequently emerge stronger than competitors who haven't been tested in the same way. They develop capabilities, mind-sets, and stories that become competitive advantages in the long run.

BUSINESS LESSON: Look for the potential advantages within adver-sity. The challenges that test you today may become the strengths that distinguish you tomorrow.

MENTAL TOUGHNESS

In basketball, mental toughness is as important as physical ability—espe-cially when facing adversity. The players who can stay focused under pressure, who can maintain confidence through slumps, who can control their emotions in heated moments—these are the players coaches want on the floor when the game is on the line.

The same quality is crucial for entrepreneurs navigating business chal-lenges. Mental toughness in business includes:

- Maintaining perspective during crises
- Managing emotions so they inform decisions without controlling them
- Focusing on controllable factors rather than circumstances beyond your influence
- Bouncing back quickly from disappointments
- Sustaining effort and optimism through extended difficult periods

"A lot of us was taught that pro, you can only go pro whether you become a rapper or a basketball player," I point out. This limited mindset creates fragility—if those specific paths don't work out, you're left without direction or confidence.

Mental toughness comes from a broader, more resilient mindset: "The word pro means professional. Being a person that's looked at as a legend, and everybody knows you... sometimes you find yourself following others. I'm a ballplayer, I'm not a rapper, but I followed the rappers."

Recognizing my authentic path rather than following others' expectations was a crucial element of mental toughness for me. It allowed me to redefine success on my own terms rather than feeling defeated when one narrow definition didn't materialize.

BUSINESS LESSON: Develop mental toughness through perspective, authenticity, and emotional management. Your mindset often determines whether challenges defeat you or develop you.

SUPPORT SYSTEMS

Even the greatest basketball players don't overcome adversity alone. They rely on coaches who help them adjust their approach, teammates who encourage them through difficult moments, family members who provide perspective and support, and mentors who share wisdom from their own experiences.

In business, support systems are equally important. The entrepreneurs who try to navigate adversity alone often struggle longer and recover more slowly than those who leverage the right support:

- Mentors who provide guidance based on their own experiences
- Peers who offer encouragement and understanding
- Advisors who contribute expertise in specific areas
- Family members who provide emotional support and perspective
- Professional resources (coaches, therapists, consultants) who offer structured assistance

"I believe that it's a reason why God has us connected with the people that we are connected to in our life," I reflect. "It's just for us to figure that out and get on the right track and make those things work to our benefit."

The key is not just having support but being willing to activate it—to acknowledge when you need help, to ask specific questions, to be vulnerable about challenges, to receive guidance with openness. Many entrepreneurs, especially those from communities like mine where self-reliance is highly valued, struggle with this vulnerability. But overcoming this resistance creates access to resources that can dramatically accelerate recovery from setbacks.

BUSINESS LESSON: Build and leverage support systems before and during adversity. The right guidance at the right moment can transform how you navigate challenges.

THE POWER OF PATIENCE

In basketball, some of the most impressive comebacks happen gradually—one possession at a time, one stop at a time, one basket at a time. The teams that try to erase a 20-point deficit with a single play usually dig themselves deeper. The teams that methodically chip away at the lead, staying patient and focused, are the ones that complete the comeback.

In business recovery, patience is equally important. When facing significant setbacks, the entrepreneurs who try to fix everything immediately often make things worse. Those who take a patient, methodical approach—addressing root causes rather than just symptoms, rebuilding foundations before adding structure, allowing time for new approaches to gain traction—are more likely to achieve sustainable recovery.

"I set my goals by really taking my time," I explain. "I've worked on my patience. I try not to force things that I would understand from building with God that is already for me. And I used to do that a lot. But whatever's for you is never forced."

This patience isn't passive—it's strategic. It's about moving at the right pace rather than the fastest possible pace. It's about recognizing that sustainable solutions often take longer to implement but create more lasting results.

"Your timing versus God's timing is two different timings," I remind people. "What's to come is better than what's going, and if you give Him a shot... whatever it was that you wanted, when you learn patience, what God gave you, you knew it was 5-10 times better than what you could have expected."

BUSINESS LESSON: Practice strategic patience during recovery. The most sustainable comebacks aren't usually the fastest ones.

CREATING YOUR COMEBACK STRATEGY: THE PLAYBOOK

Now it's time to develop your own approach to navigating adversity and creating comebacks when necessary. Here's a structured framework for turning setbacks into comebacks:

1. **Adversity Preparation:** Before specific challenges arise, build the foundation for effective response:
    - Identify potential vulnerabilities in your business
    - Develop contingency plans for likely scenarios
    - Build financial reserves that create response options
    - Establish support systems you can activate when needed
    - Cultivate the mindset that sees adversity as developmental
2. **Initial Response Protocol:** When adversity strikes, follow a structured approach to the immediate situation:
    - Acknowledge the reality without minimizing or catastrophizing
    - Assess the specific impact and implications

- ○ Communicate appropriately with stakeholders
- ○ Stabilize the situation to prevent further deterioration
- ○ Create space for strategic rather than reactive decisions

3. **Root Cause Analysis:** Move beyond symptoms to understand underlying issues:
   - ○ Identify what factors contributed to the adversity
   - ○ Distinguish between external circumstances and internal factors
   - ○ Look for patterns that might indicate systemic issues
   - ○ Consider multiple perspectives on what happened and why
   - ○ Document insights for future prevention and response

4. **Reinvention Planning:** Develop a structured approach to necessary changes:
   - ○ Clarify what core elements must be preserved
   - ○ Identify specific aspects that need to evolve
   - ○ Research potential new approaches and models
   - ○ Test hypotheses in small ways before full commitment
   - ○ Create implementation roadmaps for significant changes

5. **Recovery Execution:** Implement your comeback strategy methodically:
   - ○ Break the recovery into manageable phases
   - ○ Define clear milestones to track progress
   - ○ Communicate the plan to maintain stakeholder confidence
   - ○ Adjust approaches based on feedback and results
   - ○ Celebrate small wins to maintain momentum

6. **Support Activation:** Leverage appropriate resources at each stage:

○ Identify specific needs where support would add value

○ Match needs with the right support sources

○ Frame clear requests rather than general calls for help

○ Receive support with openness and appreciation

○ Reciprocate when possible to strengthen relationships

7. **Learning Integration:** Extract and apply lessons from the experience:

○ Document key insights while they're fresh

○ Identify specific changes to prevent similar issues

○ Share relevant learnings with your team and network

○ Create systems to apply these lessons going forward

○ Reframe the experience as development rather than just difficulty

Remember, comebacks aren't just about returning to where you were before adversity struck. They're about emerging stronger, wiser, and better positioned than you were previously. The goal isn't just recovery—it's transformation.

COURT TO BUSINESS: COMEBACK APPLICATION

On the Court	In Business
Adjusting game strategy when behind	Pivoting business model when needed
Playing through injury	Continuing despite personal challenges
Bouncing back after a tough loss	Recovering from business setbacks

Off-season development	Using downtime for skill building
Comeback from point deficit	Turnaround from business decline
Veteran leadership in crisis	Experienced guidance during challenges

REAL TALK WITH A-BUTTA

I started my podcast in 2016 and didn't get sponsorship until 2024. That's eight years of putting in work with no guarantee it would ever pay off. Eight years of believing in a vision when there was little external validation. Eight years of reinventing myself when it would have been easier to just rely on my basketball reputation.

"Getting into a lane and doing something not really knowing, in this entrepreneurship world versus really getting a job and having a 401(k), to really think about a retirement knowing you got kids—these choices ain't easy," I admit.

But the determination I had on the court became my mindset off the court. "I've always told myself that if I became a legend on the court, there's no way you can tell me I can't become one off the court," I explain.

That belief sustained me through the doubts, through the slow progress, through the moments when it seemed like nothing was happening. It kept me showing up, creating content, building relationships, developing skills—doing the work even when results weren't immediate or visible.

And that's what I want to pass on to you: Adversity doesn't mean you're on the wrong path. Setbacks don't mean your vision is flawed. The need to reinvent doesn't mean you've failed.

These challenges are part of every significant journey. They're not exceptions to the process—they're essential elements of it. The fire that seems to be destroying you is actually forging you into something stronger, something more resilient, something more unique and valuable than you were before.

"From all of the traveling with basketball and I've seen in the world, for me to say where I know that I came from and I'm still here, I can never say that Harlem means everything to me because I've been exposed to so much, but Harlem means a lot to me that I want to be able to help give that back from what I've been exposed to."

That's the ultimate comeback—not just recovering from adversity but using what it taught you to lift others. When you can take your hardest moments and transform them into wisdom that helps the next generation navigate their challenges more effectively—that's when you know you've truly turned a setback into a setup for something greater than you could have imagined before.

The game isn't over. Your story isn't finished. The comeback is still being written. And the best chapters may be the ones that follow your greatest challenges.

CHAPTER 9

THE ASSIST - MENTORSHIP AND GIVING BACK

"If it's one thing that I want to stress, man, fathers don't give up on your kids. No matter what you go through, don't give up on these kids. My hood never seen me give up on my kids. They never seen me not outside with my girls and my children. No matter what my relationships was, you never seen me bashing my baby mothers or talking bad about them. A girl just needs her dad."*

In basketball, the assist might be the most underrated statistic. Highlight reels focus on dunks and three-pointers, but the pass that created the opportunity often goes unnoticed. Yet the greatest players understand that assists are as valuable as baskets—they create opportunities for others to succeed and elevate the entire team's performance.

In business and life, the same principle applies. True success isn't just about what you accomplish individually—it's about how you help others succeed, how you create opportunities for the next generation, how you pass on what you've learned so that others can go even further.

This chapter is about the assist—how to mentor others effectively, how to give back to your community, how to create opportunities for those coming behind you, and how to build a legacy that extends beyond your own achievements.

THE MENTORSHIP MINDSET

Throughout my journey, mentors have played crucial roles at different stages. Some were formal coaches, others were community leaders, and still others were simply older players who took time to share their knowledge and perspective.

"Rest in peace, my man Lex," I remember. "He ran St. Mark's. He called me a gym rat. He just wanted me to always stay in the gym. And I never understood why someone used to say, 'Close to Lenox, you live on Seventh, you need to come down between Lenox and Fifth and live in this gym.'"

Looking back, I realize what this mentor was really doing—he wasn't just pushing me to improve my basketball skills. He was creating a safe space for me to develop, keeping me focused on positive activities, instilling discipline and work ethic that would serve me far beyond the court.

This is the essence of mentorship—seeing potential in someone that they might not yet see in themselves, and helping them develop that potential through guidance, opportunity, and sometimes challenging them beyond their comfort zone.

The mentorship mindset includes:

- Looking for potential rather than just current ability

- Taking a long-term view of someone's development
- Sharing knowledge without expectation of immediate return
- Creating opportunities that might not otherwise exist
- Offering both support and appropriate challenge
- Seeing others' success as an extension of your own legacy

"I'm an extension of that for my pastor," I explain. "They don't go to church, and I don't judge people on that, but I know how to speak the words that I'm hearing from my pastor to the streets. They can relate like this. And I'm still saying the same words that come out the Bible. I'm just not saying it like him."

This chain of mentorship—receiving wisdom from one source and adapting it to reach others in a way that resonates with their reality—is how knowledge and wisdom spread and grow across generations and communities.

BUSINESS LESSON: Develop a mentorship mindset that looks for opportunities to help others grow. The impact of your success multiplies when you help others succeed.

IDENTIFYING MENTORSHIP OPPORTUNITIES

Mentorship doesn't always happen through formal programs or official relationships. Often, the most impactful mentorship happens through natural connections where you recognize an opportunity to make a difference.

In my life, I look for mentorship opportunities in several contexts:

- Young people in my community who show potential but lack guidance
- Team members who could develop into leadership roles with the right support
- Family members navigating challenges I've already experienced
- Entrepreneurs facing obstacles I've overcome
- Anyone demonstrating hunger for growth and willingness to learn

The key is recognizing where your specific experience, knowledge, and perspective could benefit someone else's journey. This isn't about positioning yourself as having all the answers—it's about sharing the specific wisdom you've gained through your particular path.

"I want to show examples of other ways to go pro," I share when talking about my podcast and other projects. "I know Fat Joe or Joe King went pro. But when I look at you, I look at Rashad, everybody went pro. And again, those are all examples of what? Never giving up."

By highlighting diverse examples of success—different paths to "going pro" in life—I'm providing mentorship that expands possibilities for young people who might otherwise see very limited options.

BUSINESS LESSON: Look for organic mentorship opportunities where your specific experience can benefit others. Effective mentorship matches your knowledge with another's needs.

EFFECTIVE MENTORING APPROACHES

Not all mentorship is equally effective. The approach that works with one person might not work with another. The methods that are appropriate at one stage of development might be counterproductive at another stage.

Some mentoring approaches I've found effective include:

- Sharing stories that illustrate principles rather than just stating the principles
- Asking questions that promote self-discovery rather than always providing answers
- Creating opportunities for hands-on experience rather than just theoretical knowledge
- Providing honest feedback delivered with genuine care
- Modeling the behaviors and mindsets you're trying to instill
- Connecting mentees with resources and networks beyond your own

"I try not to bring people outside of where they would have to work or do a little bit more than who they are," I explain when discussing how I position people for success. This principle applies to mentorship as well—effective mentoring meets people where they are and helps them grow from that starting point, rather than trying to force them into a predefined mold.

BUSINESS LESSON: Adapt your mentoring approach to the individual and situation. Effective mentorship is personalized, not standardized.

THE FATHERHOOD IMPERATIVE

Of all the mentorship roles I've taken on, none is more important than being a father to my children. This is a responsibility that transcends all others and shapes not just individual lives but the future of our communities.

"A lot of fathers go through a lot of ups and downs, trying to understand their love for their child versus the love that they have in a relationship," I acknowledge. But despite those challenges, I've made it a priority to remain consistently present and supportive for my children.

"My hood never seen me give up on my kids," I state with pride. "They never seen me not outside with my girls and my children. No matter what my relationships was, you never seen me bashing my baby mothers or talking bad about them."

This commitment isn't just about personal family values—it's about breaking cycles of absence and disconnection that have impacted our communities for generations. It's about showing the next generation a different model of manhood, responsibility, and love.

The principles that make for effective fatherhood also apply to other mentorship contexts:

- Consistent presence that builds trust over time
- Unconditional support that doesn't depend on performance
- Boundaries and expectations that provide structure
- Guidance that balances protection with growing independence
- Modeling the values you hope to instill

"No matter how old she may be, a girl just needs her dad," I emphasize. This truth—that our presence and engagement matter profoundly to those we mentor—applies across all mentoring relationships.

BUSINESS LESSON: Approach mentorship with the same commitment and consistency you would bring to parenting. The most impactful mentoring relationships are characterized by reliability and genuine care.

COMMUNITY IMPACT

While individual mentoring relationships are powerful, they're even more effective when embedded within broader community impact. The basketball tournaments, youth programs, and community events I've been involved with create contexts where mentorship can happen naturally and at scale.

"I want to bring Greg Marius' foundation in with me to be a part of that so we can figure something out," I explain when discussing a program for the Boys and Girls Club. "Why? Because his name holds weight and it should be connected to people who feel like, 'Hey, I want to pour into that. I used to play in Greg Marius' tournament.'"

This approach to community impact recognizes that mentorship thrives within ecosystems—networks of support, opportunity, and positive influence that reinforce each other. When young people see multiple examples of success, when they have access to diverse resources and perspectives, when they feel part of something larger than themselves—that's when transformation happens most powerfully.

Effective community impact includes:

- Creating platforms where multiple mentors can connect with those needing guidance
- Building partnerships that combine complementary strengths and resources
- Designing programs that address holistic needs rather than isolated issues
- Establishing sustainability so impact continues beyond initial enthusiasm
- Measuring outcomes to understand what's working and what needs adjustment

BUSINESS LESSON: Embed mentorship within broader community impact strategies. Individual guidance becomes more powerful when supported by community ecosystems.

RECIPROCAL LEARNING

The most effective mentorship isn't one-directional—it's reciprocal. While the mentor may have more experience in certain areas, the mentee brings fresh perspective, new questions, and different experiences that can benefit the mentor as well.

I've learned as much from those I've mentored as they've learned from me. They've helped me see blind spots in my thinking, introduced me to new ideas and technologies, challenged assumptions I didn't realize I was making, and kept me connected to evolving realities.

This reciprocal learning creates mentorship relationships that last and evolve over time, rather than being limited to a specific period or purpose. As the mentee develops, the relationship can transform into a peer connection or even reverse, with the former mentee providing guidance in areas where they've developed expertise.

"When basketball is not there anymore to bring joy to other people's lives, I got paid to play. So people paid me to play," I reflect on how relationships changed when my playing days ended. This taught me the importance of building connections based on mutual value and growth, not just on what one person can do for another.

BUSINESS LESSON: Approach mentorship as a two-way learning opportunity. The most sustainable mentoring relationships create value for both parties.

LEGACY THINKING

True mentorship is ultimately about legacy—about impact that extends beyond your direct actions to influence future generations and create lasting change.

"I've never heard street ball stories have good endings," I observe. "I never really heard street ball people really figuring out with the legendary status and the love that they get in the streets... we brag about all the people that we connected to and got love for us and respect for us, but we can't take none of that to the bank."

This recognition has driven me to think beyond immediate acclaim or recognition to build something more lasting—something that creates pathways for others, that changes narratives about what's possible, that leaves structures and systems that continue to create opportunity.

Legacy thinking includes:

- Considering the long-term impact of current decisions
- Building sustainability into programs and initiatives
- Documenting knowledge and wisdom so it can be shared broadly
- Developing leaders who can carry work forward
- Creating models that can be replicated and adapted by others

"Look at what I watched you do, and look at how I'm trying to reinvent myself and remix that," I say about honoring Greg Marius' legacy. This is the essence of legacy thinking—not just preserving what came before, but building upon it in ways that extend its impact to new contexts and generations.

BUSINESS LESSON: Think beyond immediate impact to long-term legacy. The most meaningful success creates positive change that continues beyond your direct involvement.

CREATING YOUR MENTORSHIP APPROACH: THE PLAYBOOK

Now it's time to develop your own approach to mentorship and community impact. Here's a structured framework for becoming an effective mentor and creating lasting positive influence:

1. **Mentorship Inventory:** Assess what you have to offer as a mentor:
    - Knowledge and skills from your specific experiences
    - Access to networks and opportunities you can share
    - Perspective gained from your unique journey
    - Resources (time, space, funding) you can contribute
    - Specific groups you're uniquely positioned to serve

2. **Mentorship Modalities:** Identify the approaches that best fit your strengths and availability:
   - One-on-one formal mentoring relationships
   - Group mentoring through workshops or programs
   - Content creation that shares knowledge broadly
   - Creating platforms where others can connect
   - Funding or supporting existing mentorship initiatives

3. **Mentee Identification:** Develop a thoughtful approach to selecting mentees:
   - Clear criteria based on potential impact and fit
   - Initial conversations to assess mutual benefit
   - Trial periods before longer-term commitments
   - Diversity considerations to extend opportunity
   - Balance between helping those most like you versus those most different

4. **Mentorship Structure:** Create frameworks that support effective guidance:
   - Clear expectations for both mentor and mentee
   - Regular meeting or communication schedules
   - Specific goals and milestones to track progress
   - Resources to support development between interactions
   - Boundaries that maintain healthy relationship dynamics

5. **Community Impact Strategy:** Design approaches that create broader influence:
   - Programs that address specific community needs
   - Partnerships that leverage complementary strengths
   - Funding mechanisms that ensure sustainability
   - Measurement systems that track meaningful outcomes
   - Replication models that allow scaling beyond direct involvement

6. **Knowledge Sharing Systems:** Develop ways to extend your impact through documentation:
   - Written guides or books that capture key principles
   - Video or audio content that preserves stories and lessons
   - Training programs that prepare others to mentor
   - Frameworks that make tacit knowledge explicit
   - Archives that preserve history and wisdom for future generations

7. **Legacy Planning:** Create strategies for impact that outlasts your direct involvement:
   - Leadership development to prepare succession
   - Institutional structures that can continue work
   - Endowments or funding models for long-term sustainability
   - Documentation of vision, values, and methodologies
   - Networks that will maintain connections beyond your involvement

Remember, mentorship isn't about creating clones of yourself or receiving credit for others' accomplishments. It's about helping people develop their own authentic greatness, about removing obstacles from their path, about providing guidance that allows them to go further than they could have gone alone—and perhaps further than you've gone yourself.

COURT TO BUSINESS: MENTORSHIP APPLICATION

On the Court	In Business
Veteran players guiding rookies	Experienced entrepreneurs mentoring startups

Team captains leading by example	Business leaders modeling values and practices
Coaches developing player potential	Mentors helping identify and build on strengths
Creating scoring opportunities for teammates	Opening doors and making connections for mentees
Teaching specific skills and techniques	Transferring specific knowledge and methodologies
Building team culture and standards	Establishing values and expectations

REAL TALK WITH A-BUTTA

I've come to understand that true greatness isn't measured by what you accomplish alone—it's measured by what you help others accomplish. It's not about how high you climb—it's about how many people you bring with you.

"The help is what really helps us," I explain. "Being around the help. You become the help."

This perspective transforms how we think about success. It's no longer just about personal achievement or recognition. It's about impact. It's about legacy. It's about creating ripples that continue long after we're gone.

For me, this understanding has been particularly important as a father. "I want to inspire kids by not just my story, but being connected to people that never gave up," I share. "They ain't stopped."

This is the essence of the assist—using your position, your knowledge, your connections, your story to create opportunities for others. It's recognizing that the greatest achievements aren't the ones that end with you, but the ones that begin with you and continue through those you've influenced.

As you build your business, your brand, your career, think beyond personal success to meaningful impact. Ask not just "What am I building?" but "Who am I helping to build?" Not just "What am I achieving?" but "What am I enabling others to achieve?"

Because at the end of the day, the most valuable statistic isn't how many points you scored—it's how many assists you made. It's not the applause you received, but the opportunities you created. It's not who knows your name, but whose lives are better because they crossed paths with you.

That's the true measure of a life well lived. That's the legacy worth building. That's the game worth playing.

CHAPTER 10

THE LEGACY - BUILDING SOMETHING THAT LASTS

"I *never really heard street ball stories have good endings. I never really heard street ball people really figuring out with the legendary status and the love that they get in the streets... we brag about all the people that we connected to and got love for us and respect for us, but we can't take none of that to the bank. So that's what this groundwork and hard work is about right now."*

In basketball, the greatest players aren't just measured by their statistics or even their championships. They're measured by their legacy—how they changed the game, who they influenced, what they built that continued after their playing days ended.

The same is true in business and life. True success isn't just about what you accomplish in the moment—it's about what you build that lasts, what you establish that continues to create value, what you leave behind that keeps working long after you've moved on to new challenges.

This final chapter is about legacy—how to think beyond short-term success to build something truly lasting, how to create value that transcends personal acclaim, how to establish systems and structures that continue generating opportunity for others, and how to define success in ways that matter not just today but for generations to come.

BEYOND THE APPLAUSE

One of the most important lessons I learned at Rucker was about the temporary nature of applause. When you're making plays, when you're winning games, when the crowd is chanting your name—it feels like it will last forever. But it doesn't.

"Rucker taught me that you know, not to always play for the applause," I reflect. "Because again, when I stopped playing basketball, I seen that I wasn't treated the same as I was when I was playing. People use you for your talent, and when you don't have a talent to offer them anymore, it depends on what type of person you are, whether you can handle that or not."

This reality—that applause is temporary—has profound implications for how we think about success and legacy. If you build your identity around external validation, you're constructing something fragile. If you measure your worth by temporary acclaim, you're setting yourself up for inevitable disappointment.

True legacy thinking requires looking beyond the applause to something more substantial and enduring:

- Value that exists independent of personal recognition
- Systems that continue functioning without your direct involvement

- Impact that grows rather than diminishes over time
- Contributions that solve fundamental problems rather than just treating symptoms
- Knowledge that can be transferred and applied by others

"I'll never forget that," I say about the lesson Cameron taught me: "Make sure that you always reinventing yourself. That is one person that taught me to stand for something before for anything."

This principle—standing for something meaningful rather than chasing fleeting acclaim—is at the heart of legacy building. It's about creating value rooted in purpose rather than personality, in solving problems rather than seeking spotlight.

BUSINESS LESSON: Build for lasting impact rather than temporary acclaim. True legacy transcends personal recognition to create enduring value.

GENERATIONAL WEALTH MINDSET

In the communities I come from, one of the most powerful shifts in thinking is from immediate consumption to generational wealth building. This shift changes how we view success, how we make decisions, and how we structure our enterprises.

"You can't take none of that to the bank," I emphasize when talking about street fame and connections. This stark reality has driven me to think beyond reputation to tangible value creation—building businesses, creating assets, and establishing structures that can be passed down and built upon by future generations.

The generational wealth mindset includes several key elements:

- Thinking in decades rather than days
- Building assets rather than just generating income
- Creating ownership rather than just earning compensation
- Establishing systems that can operate beyond personal involvement
- Documenting knowledge so it can be transferred effectively
- Developing multiple streams of value rather than depending on a single source

This mindset doesn't mean sacrificing present needs for future possibilities. It means making strategic decisions that serve both—meeting current requirements while building toward long-term objectives.

"I'm grateful that I've had multiple nicknames to be able to keep myself and my identity up," I share. This diversity of identity and capability has allowed me to adapt and evolve rather than being trapped in a single role or reputation. The same principle applies to business legacy—creating diverse assets and capabilities that can adapt to changing conditions over time.

BUSINESS LESSON: Develop a generational wealth mindset that builds transferable value. True legacy creates assets that can grow and evolve across generations.

SUSTAINABLE BUSINESS MODELS

Many businesses are built around the skills, connections, or personality of their founder. While this approach can create short-term success, it often limits long-term legacy potential. If the business can't function without the founder, its value and impact are inherently capped.

Building businesses with sustainable models requires different thinking:

- Creating systems that can be operated by others
- Developing intellectual property that can be licensed or transferred
- Establishing recurring revenue streams rather than just project-based income
- Building teams with capabilities that complement and eventually replace the founder's
- Creating documentation that captures key processes and knowledge

"I want to show kids and the next generation that there's other way to go pro," I explain. "A lot of us was taught that pro, you can only go pro whether you become a rapper or a basketball player. So again, being that people would say I made it in street ball, because I won't be forgotten. How do I get how do I show a kid how to do that when there's life after basketball?"

This commitment to showing sustainable paths to success—"other ways to go pro"—is at the heart of legacy business building. It's not just about personal achievement but about creating models that others can adapt and apply to their own circumstances.

BUSINESS LESSON: Design business models that can function beyond your personal involvement. Sustainable systems create more lasting impact than personality-dependent enterprises.

DOCUMENTATION AND KNOWLEDGE TRANSFER

One of the most important aspects of legacy building is documentation—capturing the knowledge, insights, and methodologies you've developed so they can be transferred to others.

This book itself is an example of documentation—taking the lessons I've learned through basketball and business and presenting them in a form that can benefit others who haven't had direct access to my experience.

Effective documentation and knowledge transfer can take many forms:

- Written materials like books, guides, and playbooks
- Video and audio content that captures demonstrations and explanations
- Training programs that systematically develop skills in others
- Mentorship structures that allow for personalized knowledge transmission
- Stories and case studies that illustrate principles in action

"I want to inspire kids by not just my story, but being connected to people that never gave up," I share. "They ain't stopped."

This approach—combining personal story with broader examples of persistence and success—creates more powerful documentation than either element alone. It connects principles to practice, theory to application, showing not just what to do but how real people have done it in real circumstances.

BUSINESS LESSON: Document your knowledge and methodologies systematically. Effective knowledge transfer extends your impact beyond direct personal interaction.

INSTITUTIONAL LEGACY

While individual mentorship and influence are powerful, institutional structures can create even more lasting impact. Organizations, foundations, programs, and platforms can continue operating and evolving long after their founders have moved on.

I've seen this reality in Harlem, where certain institutions have shaped generations of young people, providing consistent support and opportunity despite changing leadership and circumstances.

"How do I get how do I show a kid how to do that when there's life after basketball?" I ask. "And that's kind of like what I'm doing with my podcast, doing this with book, just a documentary in general about my life, that you'll never give up."

These initiatives—the podcast, this book, the documentary—represent early steps toward institutional legacy. They create platforms that can continue influencing people I'll never meet directly, sharing lessons and perspectives that might otherwise remain limited to my immediate circle.

Building institutional legacy involves:

- Creating legal and organizational structures that can outlast individual involvement
- Establishing clear mission and values that guide decision-making
- Developing leadership pipelines to ensure continuity
- Creating funding models that support sustainable operation
- Building systems for adaptation and evolution as conditions change

"I've always had this attitude that I could win," I reflect. "If I always had this attitude that I could win, and I'm a butt, and I'm this person I feel like, if I'm learning myself, you know how many people want that?"

This insight—that my experience and approach can benefit others facing similar challenges—is the foundation of institutional thinking. It recognizes that what I've learned has value beyond my personal application of it, and that creating structures to share it more broadly multiplies its impact.

BUSINESS LESSON: Build institutions that can carry your vision forward. Organizational structures create more lasting impact than individual efforts alone.

REDEFINING SUCCESS

Perhaps the most fundamental aspect of legacy building is redefining what success means—moving beyond conventional metrics like wealth, fame, or power to more meaningful and lasting measures of impact.

"I haven't let the isolation make me feel like he's forgotten about me," I share. This perspective—maintaining faith and purpose even during periods when external validation is absent—reflects a deeper definition of success than mere recognition or reward.

Redefining success might include:

- Measuring value created for others rather than just acquired for yourself
- Evaluating the sustainability of impact rather than just its immediate extent
- Considering the quality of relationships built rather than just the quantity of connections made
- Assessing development of others rather than just personal achievement
- Examining alignment with core values rather than just external metrics

"I try to make sure that I let people know that they appreciate it being thought about," I explain. "Why? Because, you know, those nights and weeks and days and months, man, when people not... y'all better start learning how to tell people, even though you didn't see it coming from them, you better start learning how to let people know you're appreciative."

This appreciation—acknowledging those who contribute to your journey even when their role isn't obvious or immediately beneficial—reflects a definition of success that includes communal well-being rather than just individual advancement.

BUSINESS LESSON: Define success in terms that promote lasting positive impact. The metrics you choose shape the legacy you build.

THE HARLEM IMPERATIVE

For me, legacy building is inseparable from my connection to Harlem—the community that shaped me, that gave me opportunities, that supported my development even as it presented challenges.

"Harlem means a lot to me because it helped me see that because I grew up in poverty, I didn't have to have a poverty mindset," I reflect. "There's so much that I see in Harlem that you can be ashamed of and hurt by, but there's so much of Harlem that you could see, wow, I didn't realize that it had this much of an impact."

This balanced perspective—recognizing both the challenges and the strengths of my community—shapes how I think about legacy. It's not about escaping or transcending where I came from. It's about building upon its strengths while addressing its challenges, about creating pathways for others while honoring the path that brought me here.

"I know that if the rest of the world has been exposed to me and have felt the way that they felt, and I've made the impact that I've made, whether it was in junior college in California or junior college in Arkansas, wherever I went, my Harlem style has touched someone in a different way," I observe. "So again, I want to be able to give that and help people that come from Harlem be able to spread that all over the world."

This commitment—to spread the positive aspects of Harlem's influence while creating new opportunities for its people—represents a community-focused approach to legacy building. It recognizes that individual success is meaningful when it contributes to collective advancement, when it opens doors not just for yourself but for those who share your origin story.

BUSINESS LESSON: Connect your legacy to community impact. The most meaningful success contributes to the advancement of the communities that shaped you.

THE FATHERHOOD LEGACY

Of all the legacies we build, none is more profound or lasting than the impact we have on our children. This truth has shaped my priorities and decisions, especially as I've transitioned from basketball to business.

"If it's one thing that I want to stress, man, fathers don't give up on your kids," I emphasize. "No matter what you go through, don't give up on these kids."

This commitment—to remain present and supportive for my children regardless of circumstances—represents the most fundamental form of legacy building. It recognizes that the values, lessons, and support we provide to our children shape not just their lives but potentially generations to come.

The fatherhood legacy includes:

- Modeling the values and behaviors you hope to instill
- Creating stability and security that builds confidence
- Providing guidance while encouraging independence
- Demonstrating healthy relationships and conflict resolution
- Building financial foundation that creates opportunity

"My hood never seen me give up on my kids," I state with pride. "They never seen me not outside with my girls and my children. No matter what my relationships was, you never seen me bashing my baby mothers or talking bad about them."

This visible commitment—being consistently present and positive despite relationship challenges—creates legacy not just within my own family but in the broader community. It demonstrates possibilities, sets expectations, and challenges narratives about fatherhood, particularly in communities where father absence has been normalized.

BUSINESS LESSON: Recognize that personal relationships, especially with children, may be your most important legacy. Balance business building with investment in family legacy.

CREATING YOUR LEGACY PLAN: THE PLAYBOOK

Now it's time to develop your own approach to building lasting legacy. Here's a structured framework for creating impact that endures beyond your direct involvement:

1. **Legacy Vision:** Define what you want your lasting impact to be:
   o Core problems you want to help solve
   o Communities you want to serve
   o Values you want to perpetuate
   o Systems you want to change or create
   o Stories you want to be told about your contribution
2. **Legacy Vehicles:** Identify the specific mechanisms for creating lasting impact:
   o Businesses with sustainable models
   o Written or recorded knowledge
   o Mentored individuals who will continue your work

- ○ Organizations or foundations
- ○ Products or services with lasting utility
- ○ Financial assets that can be transferred

3. **Sustainability Planning:** Design approaches that enable continued impact:
   - ○ Funding models that provide ongoing resources
   - ○ Leadership development for eventual succession
   - ○ Documentation of key processes and knowledge
   - ○ Legal structures that protect and perpetuate your work
   - ○ Adaptation mechanisms that allow evolution as conditions change

4. **Value Transfer Systems:** Create methods for passing on what you've built:
   - ○ Mentorship programs that develop future leaders
   - ○ Training systems that transfer critical knowledge
   - ○ Documentation that captures insights and methodologies
   - ○ Networks that connect those who will carry work forward
   - ○ Transition processes for smooth leadership changes

5. **Legacy Protection:** Develop safeguards for what you've established:
   - ○ Legal protections for intellectual property
   - ○ Governance structures that maintain mission alignment
   - ○ Financial reserves that provide stability during challenges
   - ○ Relationship networks that offer support and accountability
   - ○ Conflict resolution systems that address inevitable tensions

6. **Impact Measurement:** Create methods to assess your legacy's effectiveness:
    - Specific metrics that indicate lasting positive change
    - Feedback systems that capture both qualitative and quantitative impact
    - Regular review processes to evaluate progress
    - Adaptation mechanisms based on measurement insights
    - Documentation of both successes and failures for future learning

7. **Personal Integration:** Align your daily actions with your legacy vision:
    - Priority-setting that reflects long-term legacy goals
    - Time allocation that invests in what will last
    - Relationship building with those who will carry work forward
    - Skill development in areas critical to legacy creation
    - Regular reflection on alignment between current activity and legacy vision

Remember, legacy building isn't separate from your daily work and life—it's a perspective that infuses everything you do with longer-term thinking and broader impact consideration. It's not about delaying value creation until some future point—it's about creating immediate value in ways that can continue and compound over time.

COURT TO BUSINESS: LEGACY APPLICATION

On the Court	In Business
Records and championships	Businesses and institutions built

Playing style influence	Methodologies and approaches developed
Mentoring younger players	Developing next generation of leaders
Team culture establishment	Organizational values and systems
Community programs	Social impact initiatives
Basketball camps and clinics	Training programs and educational content

REAL TALK WITH A-BUTTA

When I look around at legends before me, I see too many stories with unhappy endings. I see talent that wasn't translated into lasting impact. I see acclaim that didn't create security. I see potential that wasn't fully realized.

And I'm determined that my story will be different.

"The stories before me, like I said, no disrespect to them, but I've never heard the street ball stories where they had good endings," I observe. "You know what I mean? It made you feel inspired and motivated to say, you know, that's what I could do too."

This is the challenge I've set for myself—to create a different narrative, to establish a new model, to show what's possible when street credibility becomes the foundation for business credibility, when basketball lessons become life lessons, when personal achievement becomes community advancement.

"A lot of us was taught that pro, you can only go pro whether you become a rapper or a basketball player," I explain. "So again, being that people would say I made it in street ball, because I won't be forgotten. How do I get how do I show a kid how to do that when there's life after basketball?"

That question—how to translate street ball success into lasting impact—has driven my journey since I stepped off the court. It's pushed me to start podcasts, write books, build businesses, mentor young people, strengthen family bonds, and create new models of success.

Because at the end of the day, legacy isn't about what people say about you when you're gone. It's about what continues working, creating value, and opening doors even when you're no longer directly involved. It's about systems, not just stories. It's about institutions, not just impressions. It's about what you build, not just what you did.

So as you take these lessons and apply them to your own journey, think beyond immediate success to lasting legacy. Ask not just "How can I win today?" but "What can I build that will still be creating value decades from now?" Not just "How can I get mine?" but "How can I create opportunity for generations to come?"

Because that's the true test of a game well played—not just the points on the scoreboard, but the impact that continues long after the final buzzer sounds. That's a whole lotta game—the kind that truly matters.

APPENDIX

THE PLAYBOOK - ESSENTIAL TOOLS FOR YOUR JOURNEY

This appendix provides practical tools, templates, and resources to help you implement the principles discussed throughout the book. Whether you're just starting your entrepreneurial journey or looking to level up an existing business, these resources will help you move from concept to execution.

FINANCIAL LITERACY FUNDAMENTALS
UNDERSTANDING THE NUMBERS THAT MATTER

Cash Flow Tracking Template

Week	Income	Expenses	Net Cash Flow	Running Balance
1				
2				
3				
4				

The Three Financial Statements You Need to Know

1. **Income Statement (Profit & Loss)**
   - Shows revenue, expenses, and profit over a period
   - Key for understanding if your business is profitable
2. **Balance Sheet**
   - Shows assets, liabilities, and equity at a point in time
   - Key for understanding your overall financial position
3. **Cash Flow Statement**
   - Shows how cash is moving in and out of your business
   - Key for understanding if you can pay your bills

5 Financial Metrics Every Entrepreneur Should Track

1. **Gross Profit Margin** = (Revenue - Cost of Goods Sold) ÷ Revenue
2. **Net Profit Margin** = Net Profit ÷ Revenue
3. **Customer Acquisition Cost (CAC)** = Marketing Expenses ÷ Number of New Customers
4. **Lifetime Value (LTV)** = Average Purchase Value × Average Purchase Frequency × Average Customer Lifespan
5. **Burn Rate** = How quickly you're spending available cash

BUILDING CREDIT AND ACCESSING CAPITAL

Steps to Build Business Credit

1. Establish your business legally (LLC, Corporation)
2. Get an EIN (Employer Identification Number)
3. Open a business bank account
4. Get a business phone number and list it

5. Apply for a D-U-N-S Number through Dun & Bradstreet
6. Open a business credit card and pay it on time
7. Establish trade lines with suppliers who report to credit bureaus
8. Monitor your business credit reports regularly

Funding Sources for New Entrepreneurs

- Personal savings
- Friends and family investment
- Small business loans
- Community development financial institutions
- Angel investors
- Crowdfunding
- Grants (especially for specific demographics or industries)
- Supplier financing
- Pre-sales and customer funding

Alternative Funding Sources to Consider

- Revenue-based financing
- Equipment leasing
- Invoice factoring
- Merchant cash advances
- Microloans
- Business plan competitions
- Incubator/Accelerator programs
- Strategic partner investment

BUSINESS PLANNING ESSENTIALS

ONE-PAGE BUSINESS PLAN TEMPLATE

Vision Statement: [What you ultimately want to accomplish]

Mission Statement: [How you'll accomplish your vision]

Value Proposition: [Why customers should choose your business]

Target Market: [Who will pay for your product/service]

Revenue Streams: [How you'll make money]

Key Activities: [Essential operations to deliver value]

Key Resources: [Assets required to deliver your offering]

Cost Structure: [Major expenses to run the business]

Success Metrics: [How you'll measure progress]

MARKET RESEARCH FRAMEWORK

Industry Analysis

- Market size and growth rate
- Key trends affecting the industry
- Major players and market share
- Regulatory considerations

Customer Analysis

- Demographics of target customers
- Psychographics (values, interests, lifestyles)
- Pain points and needs
- Buying behaviors and preferences

Competitor Analysis

- Direct competitors (same solution)
- Indirect competitors (different solution, same problem)
- Strengths and weaknesses of each competitor
- Gaps in the market not being addressed

SWOT Analysis

- Strengths (internal positives)
- Weaknesses (internal challenges)
- Opportunities (external positives)
- Threats (external challenges)

MINIMUM VIABLE PRODUCT (MVP) PLANNING

Core Problem Definition

- What specific problem are you solving?
- Who has this problem most acutely?
- How are they currently solving it?
- Why is your solution better?

Essential Features Only

- List all possible features
- Mark each as "Must Have," "Should Have," "Nice to Have," or "Won't Have"
- Focus only on "Must Have" features for your MVP

Success Metrics

- What specific data will indicate your MVP is working?
- How will you collect this data?
- What threshold indicates you should continue vs. pivot?

Feedback Collection Plan

- How will you find initial users?
- What specific questions will you ask them?
- How will you incorporate their feedback?

MARKETING AND BRANDING TOOLS

PERSONAL BRAND BLUEPRINT

Your Unique Story

- Where you came from (your roots)
- Challenges you've overcome
- Key turning points in your journey
- Lessons learned along the way
- Where you're headed (your vision)

Core Values

- List 3-5 non-negotiable principles that guide your decisions
- For each value, note a specific example of how you've demonstrated it

Unique Strengths Assessment

- What skills come naturally to you?
- What do others consistently praise about your work?
- Where have you succeeded when others typically fail?
- What combination of experiences makes your perspective unique?

Visual Identity Elements

- Colors that represent your brand personality
- Typography that reflects your brand voice
- Imagery style that supports your brand story
- Logo elements that symbolize your core identity

Brand Voice Guidelines

- Tone (formal vs. casual, serious vs. playful)
- Vocabulary (simple vs. technical, traditional vs. contemporary)
- Sentence structure (short and direct vs. flowing and descriptive)
- Topics you'll discuss vs. those you'll avoid

SOCIAL MEDIA STRATEGY PLANNER

Platform Selection Guide

- Instagram: Visual businesses, B2C products, lifestyle brands
- LinkedIn: B2B services, professional expertise, thought leadership
- TikTok: Youth-oriented brands, entertainment, education through short-form video
- YouTube: Detailed how-to content, thought leadership, brand storytelling
- Twitter: News, customer service, community engagement
- Facebook: Local businesses, community building, older demographics

Content Calendar Template

Date	Platform	Content Type	Topic	Call to Action	Notes

Content Ratio Formula

- 60% Value Content (educates or entertains)
- 25% Connection Content (builds relationship)
- 15% Promotional Content (directly sells)

Engagement Metrics to Track

- Reach (how many people see your content)
- Engagement (likes, comments, shares)
- Click-through rate (percentage who take desired action)
- Conversion rate (percentage who complete a goal)

CUSTOMER JOURNEY MAPPING

Awareness Stage

- How customers first learn about you
- Their feelings and concerns at this stage
- Key questions they're asking
- Touch points where they interact with your brand
- Metrics to track effectiveness

Consideration Stage

- Information customers need to evaluate you
- Objections they might have
- Competitors they're considering
- Touch points for deeper engagement
- Metrics to track progress

Decision Stage

- Final factors in purchasing decision
- Remaining barriers to purchase
- Support needed to complete purchase
- Touch points for conversion
- Metrics to track conversion

Retention Stage

- Post-purchase experience
- Opportunities for additional value
- Touch points for ongoing relationship
- Metrics to track loyalty and satisfaction

NETWORKING AND RELATIONSHIP BUILDING

STRATEGIC NETWORKING PLAN

Relationship Inventory

- Strong connections (people who would take your call anytime)
- Weak connections (people you know but aren't close with)
- Aspirational connections (people you want to know)
- Resource gaps (expertise or connections you need)

Networking Opportunity Assessment

Event/ Platform	Target Connections	Preparation Needed	Follow-up Plan	Priority (H/M/L)

Value-First Outreach Templates

- Cold outreach that offers value before asking for anything
- Thank you messages with specific appreciation
- Check-in messages that don't request anything
- Congratulations notes for others' accomplishments
- Introduction requests that emphasize mutual benefit

Relationship Nurturing System

- Monthly reach-outs to key connections
- Quarterly value-sharing (articles, opportunities, introductions)
- Semi-annual in-person connection when possible
- Annual review of relationship portfolio

MENTOR RELATIONSHIP DEVELOPMENT

Mentor Identification Criteria

- Has achieved what you're working toward
- Possesses specific knowledge or skills you need
- Demonstrates values alignment with your goals
- Has bandwidth for mentorship
- Communication style you respond well to

Mentorship Request Approach

- Research their background thoroughly
- Start with a specific, small request
- Demonstrate you've done your homework
- Show how you've applied their previous advice

- Be clear about time expectations

Maximizing Mentorship Meetings

- Come prepared with specific questions
- Keep meetings focused and respectful of time
- Take detailed notes
- Summarize key takeaways at the end
- Follow up with actions you've taken based on advice

Mentor Appreciation Strategies

- Implement their advice and report results
- Publicly credit them (with permission)
- Look for opportunities to support their goals
- Express specific gratitude for their impact
- Pay it forward by mentoring others

PRODUCTIVITY AND EXECUTION SYSTEMS

DAILY SUCCESS ROUTINE TEMPLATE

Morning Power Hour

- Review top priorities for the day
- Complete most important task first
- Schedule reactive activities for later
- Review key metrics and adjust plans

Focus Block Planning

Time Block	Focus Area	Specific Tasks	Potential Distractions	Prevention Plan
9 - 1 1 AM				
1-3 PM				
4-5 PM				

Energy Management Framework

- High Energy: Creative work, difficult decisions, important conversations
- Medium Energy: Administrative tasks, routine meetings, planning
- Low Energy: Email processing, organization, passive learning

End-of-Day Wrap-Up

- Review accomplishments against priorities
- Identify unfinished items for tomorrow
- Document any insights or learnings
- Prepare workspace for tomorrow's start
- Transition ritual to end work mode

GOAL ACHIEVEMENT SYSTEM

90-Day Goal Framework

- One primary goal that would transform your business

- 3-5 supporting goals that enable the primary goal
- Key results that will indicate success
- Weekly milestones to track progress
- Potential obstacles and mitigation strategies

Weekly Review Process

- Progress assessment against 90-day goals
- Celebration of wins (no matter how small)
- Identification of stuck points
- Adjustment of approach based on learnings
- Setting of specific targets for coming week

Accountability Structures

- Accountability partner check-in template
- Public commitment mechanisms
- Progress tracking visualization
- Consequence and reward system
- Team alignment approach

DECISION-MAKING FRAMEWORK

Decision Classification Matrix

- Type 1 (Irreversible, high impact): Requires thorough analysis
- Type 2 (Reversible, any impact): Make quickly and adjust
- Type 3 (Low impact, any reversibility): Delegate or use rules

Key Decision Documentation Template

- Decision required:
- Deadline for decision:
- Options considered:
- Pros and cons of each:
- Information needed vs. available:
- Decision made and rationale:
- Implementation plan:
- Review date:

Decision Review Process

- Regular review of past decisions
- Assessment of outcomes vs. expectations
- Documentation of learnings
- Adjustment of decision-making approach
- Application to future decisions

LEADERSHIP AND TEAM BUILDING

TEAM MEMBER SELECTION FRAMEWORK

Role Design Template

- Core responsibilities
- Required skills and experience
- Cultural attributes needed
- Success metrics for the role
- Growth path within organization

Structured Interview Questions

- Experience validation questions
- Problem-solving scenario questions
- Values alignment questions
- Team fit questions
- Self-awareness questions

Reference Check Framework

- Specific performance questions
- Character assessment questions
- Work style and preferences
- Challenges and growth areas
- Direct experience with specific requirements

Trial Project Design

- Scope that demonstrates key skills
- Clear deliverables and timeline
- Evaluation criteria aligned with role
- Fair compensation for work
- Integration with actual business needs

TEAM DEVELOPMENT SYSTEM

Individual Growth Plans

- Current assessment of strengths and growth areas
- Specific development goals
- Learning resources and opportunities

- Application projects for new skills
- Feedback and assessment approach

Team Communication Framework

- Daily quick updates
- Weekly alignment meetings
- Monthly deeper discussions
- Quarterly strategic reviews
- Communication tools and protocols

Conflict Resolution Process

- Issue identification without blame
- Perspective sharing with active listening
- Joint problem-solving approach
- Agreement documentation
- Follow-up and reassessment

Recognition and Motivation System

- Individual recognition preferences
- Team celebration rituals
- Performance-based incentives
- Intrinsic motivation support
- Career development pathways

ADDITIONAL RESOURCES

RECOMMENDED READING

Business Fundamentals

- "The Lean Startup" by Eric Ries
- "The E-Myth Revisited" by Michael E. Gerber
- "Profit First" by Mike Michalowicz
- "Building a StoryBrand" by Donald Miller
- "The $100 Startup" by Chris Guillebeau

Personal Development

- "Mindset" by Carol Dweck
- "Atomic Habits" by James Clear
- "Deep Work" by Cal Newport
- "Grit" by Angela Duckworth
- "The Obstacle Is the Way" by Ryan Holiday

Leadership and Team Building

- "Leaders Eat Last" by Simon Sinek
- "The Five Dysfunctions of a Team" by Patrick Lencioni
- "Radical Candor" by Kim Scott
- "Drive" by Daniel Pink
- "Dare to Lead" by Brené Brown

Marketing and Sales

- "This Is Marketing" by Seth Godin
- "Influence" by Robert Cialdini

- "They Ask, You Answer" by Marcus Sheridan
- "Contagious" by Jonah Berger
- "Building a Brand Story" by Donald Miller

DIGITAL TOOLS FOR ENTREPRENEURS

Productivity and Organization

- Notion (all-in-one workspace)
- Trello or Asana (project management)
- Google Workspace (email, documents, calendar)
- Calendly (scheduling)
- Evernote or OneNote (note-taking)

Marketing and Sales

- Canva (graphic design)
- Mailchimp or ConvertKit (email marketing)
- Buffer or Hootsuite (social media management)
- Google Analytics (website analytics)
- HubSpot (CRM and marketing)

Financial Management

- QuickBooks or FreshBooks (accounting)
- Wave (free accounting for small businesses)
- Stripe or PayPal (payment processing)
- Bench (bookkeeping service)
- Expensify (expense tracking)

Team Collaboration

- Slack or Microsoft Teams (communication)
- Zoom or Google Meet (video meetings)
- Loom (video messaging)
- Miro or Mural (visual collaboration)
- Dropbox or Google Drive (file sharing)

COMMUNITY RESOURCES FOR ENTREPRENEURS

Small Business Support Organizations

- Small Business Administration (SBA)
- SCORE (free business mentoring)
- Small Business Development Centers (SBDCs)
- Women's Business Centers
- Minority Business Development Agency

Entrepreneurial Communities

- 1 Million Cups (weekly entrepreneur presentations)
- Startup Grind (events and community)
- EO (Entrepreneurs' Organization)
- YEC (Young Entrepreneur Council)
- Industry-specific associations

Online Learning Platforms

- Coursera
- Udemy
- LinkedIn Learning

- Skillshare
- edX

Funding Resources

- Community Development Financial Institutions (CDFIs)
- Local economic development organizations
- Industry-specific grant programs
- Kiva (microloans)
- Angel investor networks

Remember, these tools and resources are starting points—adapt them to your specific situation and needs. The most important tool is your mindset: approaching challenges with creativity, persistence, and a willingness to learn from both successes and failures.

As you build your business, remember the lessons from the court: prepare thoroughly, execute consistently, adapt when necessary, build a strong team, and always keep your eye on the long game. That's how you build something that lasts—something that becomes a legacy beyond yourself.

ABOUT THE AUTHOR

Adrian "A-Butta" Walton is a legendary streetball player from Harlem, New York, whose electrifying play and unforgettable nickname "Whole Lotta Game" made him a fixture at the world-famous Rucker Park. Known for his relentless work ethic, basketball IQ, and ability to hold his own against NBA players, Adrian became one of the most respected players in New York City streetball history.

Growing up in Harlem shaped Adrian's perspective on success, resilience, and community. After dominating the concrete courts and earning his legendary status at Rucker Park, Adrian faced the challenge many athletes encounter: translating short-term fame into long-term impact. Rather than becoming another cautionary tale, he committed to reinventing himself and building a legacy beyond basketball.

Today, Adrian is an entrepreneur, mentor, podcast host, and community leader who helps young people understand that success isn't limited to sports and entertainment. His podcast features conversations with successful professionals from diverse fields, showing youth that there are many paths to "going pro" in life. Adrian remains deeply connected to Harlem while reaching audiences worldwide with his message of resilience, reinvention, and responsible leadership.

As a father and role model, Adrian is passionate about breaking cycles of absence and demonstrating what committed fatherhood looks like. His transparency about his own journey—the victories, setbacks, and lessons learned along the way—makes him a relatable and authentic voice for young people navigating their own paths to success.

Adrian believes that the principles that build champions on the court can create success in the boardroom. Through his speaking, writing, and mentoring, he translates street wisdom into business acumen, helping a new generation build not just wealth but legacy.

THE WHOLE LOTTA GAME ACADEMY

The Whole Lotta Game Academy is Adrian's comprehensive 8-week online program designed to help young entrepreneurs and athletes translate their hustle mindset into business success. This interactive course combines video lessons, live group coaching, practical assignments, and accountability systems to guide participants through building their own business playbook.

What You'll Learn:

- The Streetball Mindset for Business Success
- Personal Branding: From Street Cred to Business Credit
- Financial Literacy Fundamentals for Entrepreneurs
- Building Your Squad: Team Building and Leadership
- The Hustle: Execution and Work Ethic in Business
- The Defense: Protecting What You Build
- The Comeback: Resilience and Reinvention Strategies
- The Legacy: Creating Something That Lasts

Program Includes:

- 24 video modules with actionable frameworks
- Weekly live group coaching sessions with Adrian
- Done-for-you templates and worksheets
- Private community for peer support and networking
- Guest sessions with successful entrepreneurs from Adrian's network
- Certificate of completion and ongoing alumni benefits

The Whole Lotta Game Academy runs quarterly with limited enrollment to ensure personalized attention. Scholarships are available for promising young entrepreneurs from underserved communities.

THE RUCKER ROUNDTABLE COMMUNITY

The Rucker Roundtable is Adrian's exclusive membership community for entrepreneurs committed to building businesses with streetball principles. This ongoing support system provides the accountability, resources, and connections needed to turn business vision into reality.

Community Benefits:

- Monthly virtual masterminds with Adrian and guest experts
- Quarterly business strategy sessions
- Access to a private network of like-minded entrepreneurs
- Resource library of templates, scripts, and frameworks
- Dedicated accountability partners and progress tracking
- Priority access to in-person events and retreats
- Opportunities to be featured on Adrian's podcast
- Exclusive discounts on other Whole Lotta Game offerings

The Rucker Roundtable maintains a carefully curated membership to ensure quality interactions and meaningful relationships. New members are accepted quarterly through an application process that assesses not just business potential but alignment with community values of authenticity, generosity, and commitment to excellence.

THE LEGACY BUILDER PROGRAM

For entrepreneurs serious about creating businesses that will generate generational wealth, Adrian offers The Legacy Builder Program—an intensive 6-month 1:1 coaching experience. This high-touch program is designed for established entrepreneurs looking to scale their business, elevate their leadership, and create sustainable systems for long-term impact.

Program Components:

- Comprehensive business assessment and strategic planning
- Bi-weekly 1:1 coaching sessions with Adrian
- On-call support for time-sensitive decisions
- Quarterly in-person strategy days in New York City
- Custom resource development for your specific business
- Network introductions to strategic partners and mentors
- Team alignment sessions to ensure organizational coherence
- Legacy planning for personal and business continuity

The Legacy Builder Program accepts just 6 clients per year, ensuring Adrian can provide the depth of support needed for transformational results. Clients typically have established businesses generating at least $250,000 in annual revenue and are committed to creating impact beyond financial success.

SPEAKING AND WORKSHOPS

Adrian delivers high-energy keynotes and workshops that translate streetball wisdom into practical business and life strategies. His signature talks include:

- **Court Vision: Seeing Business Opportunities Others Miss**
- **The Crossover: Reinventing Yourself for Lasting Success**
- **Street Cred to Business Credit: Building an Authentic Personal Brand**

- **The Assist: Mentorship as a Competitive Advantage**
- **Defense Wins Championships: Protecting What You've Built**

Adrian's presentations can be customized for corporate audiences, educational institutions, sports organizations, and community programs. His unique ability to connect with audiences from diverse backgrounds makes him particularly effective for organizations looking to bridge cultural divides and inspire authentic leadership.

For more information on Adrian's programs or to book him for speaking engagements, visit www.AWholelottaGame.com or email team@wholelottagame.com.